Veteran journalist **Rashmi Saksena** is a pioneer amongst women newsgatherers. She became the third woman reporter in Delhi and the city's first woman crime reporter when she joined the *Hindustan Times* in 1971. She has worked with *The Sunday Mail, The Telegraph* and *The Week*. She is currently Consulting Editor of *The Hitavada* and on the Editorial Advisory Board of *India Review & Analysis*, a journal of the think tank, Society for Policy Studies. Her awards include the Prabha Dutt Memorial Award for Balanced Reporting, the Lions Club Award for reporting Punjab insurgency and the Women of Substance Award for Journalism by Ryan Foundation.

PRAISE FOR THE BOOK

'An honest and sympathetic narrative on the lives of women drawn into the dark world of terrorism and insurgency...Rashmi Saksena records the journeys of women from deeply conservative backgrounds to the very frontlines of violent combat—and back—to uncover their passions, motives and beliefs.' —Ajai Sahni, Founding Member and Executive Director of the Institute for Conflict Management

'Saksena lets the women's voices dominate. She does not judge them for their decisions or paint them as victims who were forced into something against their wishes...an interesting and readable book.' —R. Krithika, *The Hindu*

'Painstakingly researched and brilliantly written...[these] stories encapsulate an India we know and leave unseen. This book is a gritty testament of one's sisters in arms and their impossible journey.' —Nandita Bose, *New Indian Express*

'*She Goes to War* presents us with a vivid description of women who display exceptional courage in the face of extreme danger...the accounts are gripping and all-too-real.' —*Business Line*

'The book is a delight to read not just for the sheer excellence of choosing a concept so rare but also picking up minute details that pushed these women into the unthinkable.' —*Legal Notes*

SHE GOES TO WAR

Women Militants of India

Rashmi Saksena

SPEAKING TIGER

SPEAKING TIGER BOOKS LLP
125A, Ground Floor, Shahpur Jat, near Asiad Village,
New Delhi 110049

First published in hardback by Speaking Tiger 2018
This edition first published in paperback by Speaking Tiger 2022

ISBN: 978-93-5447-094-3
eISBN: 978-93-87693-45-6

10 9 8 7 6 5 4 3 2 1

Typeset in Garamond Premier Pro by SÜRYA, New Delhi
Printed at Shree Maitrey Printech Pvt. Ltd., Noida

For my late father Inder Sahai, who instilled in me a love for the written word and a spirit of enquiry, subsequently rejoicing when I broke into what was then an all-male citadel—the newsroom of an English daily—to become a reporter.

AND

For my grandson Ayaan, who at six, is already quite a wordsmith!

Contents

Author's Note

THEY STARTED TO CROSS MY PATH IN THE MID 1990S. AS I chased news stories across the country, ranging from political to human interest, they were there. They came in various avatars. Killers, victims, mercenaries, lured innocents, misguided youth, double agents and even as the bewitched following their love to the end. On dusty trails of election campaigns across regions of Madhya Pradesh, now renamed Chhattisgarh, they were the girls the rebel Maoists had drafted into their cadres. In the remote villages of the earthquake-devastated Kashmir Valley they were conduits for Pakistan-based terror groups routing money, blankets and food to the devastated, to show sympathy for the locals. In Andhra Pradesh they were pragmatic daughters of starving handloom weavers who had exchanged a kitchen fire gone cold for two square meals in the forest camps of outlawed Naxals. At times they were the bold ones who had taken up the gun for an ideological armed struggle to overthrow elected authority. They stood large in the ranks of resistance movements in India's northeastern states of Assam, Manipur and Nagaland.

They stared down at me from posters pinned to trees or stuck to walls of ramshackle tea shops. They looked up at me from stamp-size photographs in musty police files. They jumped out of itsy-bitsy newspaper reports. They cropped up in my conversations with administrators, security personnel and intelligence gatherers. They brushed past me in courtrooms. They demanded attention as protagonists in local tales of suspicious activity, spunk and romance. Tantalizing as they were, I could not go after them simply because they were not my story of the day. Or should they have been? After following the news flash of the assassination of former Prime Minister Rajiv Gandhi, I had worked frantically to garner details of Dhanu, his assassin. She was the first known human bomb in India. I had barely spent a day on the 24-year-old when it emerged that she was an LTTE (Liberation Tigers of Tamil Eelam) operative. The story moved out of my city. I was left wondering what this woman, who had so calmly bent down to touch Rajiv Gandhi's feet seconds before detonating the belt of explosives hidden in her kurta and hours earlier had devoured a huge portion of her favourite chicken biryani, was really like. I had also noted that another woman, Nalini, was an accomplice and standby at the Sriperumbudur site of the assassination.

I had also made a mental note of the alleged role of a Kashmiri woman, Farida Dar, in the May 1996 bomb blast in New Delhi's busy Lajpat Nagar area and of another Srinagar-based woman, Anjum Zamarud Habib, who had stirred a diplomatic crisis when she was apprehended in February 2003 after she had allegedly been given money by a senior diplomat in the Pakistan High Commission to fund terrorist groups in the Valley. Stored away in my mind's file on women militants operating in India was Ishrat Jahan who was killed by the police on the outskirts of Ahmedabad, Gujarat, on 15 June 2004. According to the police she was part of a team planning to kill Prime Minister Narendra Modi then the chief minister of Gujarat. Later it was alleged that she could well have been a suicide bomber working on orders of the Lashkar-e-Taiba (LeT), the Pakistan-based terror group known to target India.

However sketchy my introduction to women insurgents in

India had been, I could not forget these figures lurking in the shadows. They refused to be trashed from memory as redundant information picked up on my journalistic travels. Their brief mentions, references made in passing and their sketchy stories were like enticing blurbs of a book or the trailer of a mystery movie or a new drink aggressively advertised, beckoning to be savoured when time permitted. I flagged them to pursue some day.

I began my chase in August 2015 just before women militants started to make international headlines as never before.

The generic term, women militants, told me little about them as persons or the lives they led. What I had read or heard about them had merely boxed them under the terrorist label. I was curious to discover the person behind a bomb explosion, an ambush, a courier ferrying arms or missives and delivering recruitment spiels. I was fascinated by these women who were trekking an unconventional path from the gender point of view, considering that they came from traditional backgrounds and social milieu. I wanted to meet them and ask them umpteen questions that would help me understand them as persons. Why had they traded the security of home and family for a life of risk and physical hardship? Were they rebels against a system that put them in a slot? Was it really a choice to break out of the traditional societal mould cast for them or was it merely coming to terms with an existence in which options were a luxury they could not afford? Were they romantics heady on ideology or simply free-spirited adventurists? What or who had motivated them to exchange the sari for army fatigues? Was it money, fear or favour done for a dear one? Did they know what they had bargained for when they took up the gun, committed to kill on order and put their lives on the line as they carried out assigned tasks? What for them fell in the line of duty? Were they aware of the fate that awaited them if apprehended, arrested and convicted? Did they know how vulnerable they were, once on the radar of law enforcement agencies? What was life like in the cadre of an underground organization? Did it mean empowerment and status as equals with the men, something which had eluded them in life overground? Were they heroines for their families and people they had left behind back home or viewed as women gone astray? Was joining banned movements a one-way street? What did 'going back' hold for them?

When I began my search for women from underground outfits they became as elusive as they had been obvious before I went looking for them. I returned to those who had spoken about them but the leads went cold. The girls were either lost to them or dead. But I did get lucky in a few cases. My chase took me to places still in the grip of insurgency as well as those where it was petering off. Here I came up against a wall. Those who knew of one-time women insurgents did not want to point them out for fear of treading on toes or courting trouble from active outfits. The code of conduct was live and let live. The one-time players seemed determined to let their monochromatic present mask their colourful past. Painstakingly, I searched police and court records, worked sources and, using them as links in a chain, established contact with about 100 women from the ranks of resistance movements in Kashmir, Chhattisgarh, Manipur, Assam and Nagaland. I enjoyed getting to know them, hearing their stories, and the time spent with them. I have selected sixteen profiles because each represents a different personality and highlights the varied sort of work they do as women militants.

Tracing them was only part of the two-year exercise. The bigger challenge was to get them talking. Suspicion and caution were what they had lived and survived by underground. It was ingrained in them and had become part of their personality. Even when I saw a chink in their protective cloak, holding promise of their opening up, it often disappeared quickly. But once they started to ask me questions about myself I knew I stood a chance. I knew they were checking me out...a habit cultivated during days of hiding. When I passed scrutiny it was always rewarding. Over many meetings, they shared their stories with no full stops. I am grateful to these women for letting me into their world which they have now put behind them, some with regret, others, happily. Their stories and the texture of their personalities vary, but the single dominant trait they have in common is to fearlessly take a chance. They did it with me. With no one to stand guarantee that I was not there to sell them out, they looked me over and agreed to be part of my book. I hope I have not let them down when I paint their portraits.

Introduction

WOMEN HAVE BECOME AN INTEGRAL PART OF INSURGENCIES across the world, playing a crucial role in both covert and overt operations. Rebel leaders started recruiting and using women operators in underground militant operations when they were still off the radar of those in the business of counter-terrorism.

The story is no different in the theatres of armed uprisings in India. The role of women cadres in insurgent organizations operating in various parts of the country, has evolved over the years—from sympathizers, activists, providers of logistical support and propaganda agents to armed fighters. Now they kill, assassinate, cradle sophisticated arms, secrete guns and dossiers, rob banks, ambush security forces and play the game of subterfuge with amazing elan. They provide cover to their male comrades when they have to emerge over-ground to travel.

Women arouse less suspicion than men and are therefore effective as couriers, informers, money collectors, intelligence-gatherers motivators and recruiters and movers of militants from one hideout to another. They travel with them posing as a wife, daughter, aunt or any relative when the men have to be in public spaces to use buses, trains and cars to move from one hideout to another. At times they include them in their family group on an outing.

They are adept at guise and guile—managing to extricate themselves out of tricky situations by hoodwinking forces at security check posts, during police search operations and even at locations of confrontation. They have excelled in combat as well. Their unhesitating use of firearms has surprised security forces, sometimes with fatal consequences for them. They are disciplined fighters, use sophisticated arms with confidence and shoot to kill without flinching.

This book is the story of Indian women militants in insurgencies in Assam, Manipur, Nagaland, Chhattisgarh and Kashmir. Although these women come from diverse regions, cultures, backgrounds and societies governed by radically different social norms, they have much in common: firstly, the conflict-drenched times in their native places has played the potter in their lives, moulding them as rebels, insurgents, militants or terrorists. Another commonality is that they have been propelled into rebellion because their menfolk have been beaten, killed, tortured or intimidated by security forces and government agents. Nothing pushes women more into subversion than the notion that injustice has been meted out to their sons, brothers, husbands and fathers.

Most of them have worked underground in hostile jungle camps or as operatives living a dual life over-ground. Also in common is the spirit to be their own person, configure their lives, take ownership of their unorthodox decisions and carry them through with grit without a thought for the consequences. Fear, panic and regret do not find space in their range of emotions. Once they join a banned outfit they see it as a job to which they must give their best to be able to live another day.

The book attempts to get under their skin and fathom what goes into the making of a woman militant. It is a peek into her mindset as she deviates from the traditional role for girls to enter the dangerous world of clandestine lethal operations and embrace the uncertain life of an insurgent. Once they sign up as militants, they take commands without questioning and execute assignments with a steely resolve. They put their lives on the line without a second thought. They have become indispensable for banned militant insurgent organizations. As foot soldiers in these organizations, they have been on the frontlines, challenging security agencies in combat. They have proved to be effective recruiters for underground outfits, motivating civilians with remarkable rhetoric. Yet, only a handful of them are ranked personnel in the hierarchy and have actually led operations; in exceptional cases, they sit at the table as policy-makers.

Their exploits are testimony to the extraordinary power of women to keep alive an underground movement. They get away where their male counterparts cannot, simply because the army and paramilitary forces involved in front-line anti-terrorist operations still lack on-the-spot facilities to frisk, detain and arrest women suspects for sustained interrogation.

Women are acutely aware of the fact that they have a shelf life of about five to eight years as militants. If they are not killed in action or captured by security forces, they face the challenge of age. As they cross into their thirties, they realize they are not as quick and alert as before. Their ability to cope with the gruelling camp life also starts to flag. They are then ready to move on and return to the once abandoned 'normal' world, to apolitical domesticity. Their lives have come full circle.

The new challenge they confront is to recast their lives as homemakers and above all, life-givers instead of life-takers. As they reappraise their lives, they push their past behind them, much as they revel in it. Their paramount desire is to become mothers and once again a cohesive part of their original milieu. But they can never forget the moment they crossed over from their prosaic lives as traditional village girls for the world of militancy.

The book presents case studies without being judgemental and with no political overtones. Political or ideological references are only in the context of the case study. The book aims to dispel preconceived notions about women militants. They are not wholly victims pleading for pity nor are they all Mata Haris or female Che Guevaras. For them being an insurgent is just a chapter in their lives, to be lived at its best, as the stories of sixteen women profiled in the book will bear out. These are not conventional interviews but insights and information culled over several meetings with them.

Most of them had no qualms about disclosing their personal details. Some agreed to meet only on the precondition of secrecy. So their names and the names of places of meetings have been changed. This does not take away from bringing to light the varied types of work women militants undertake. Their lives provide a better understanding of those who have turned overground agents or donned jungle fatigues, opting to live by the gun, either gunning down people or saving themselves from being gunned down, and eventually returning home.

The maxim 'once a killer always a killer', I believe, should not be applied to women terrorists. The book brings to fore that for them being a terrorist is merely a phase in their lives, readily given up as soon as an alternative presents itself. They are 'dyed' to become killers, just as white yarn is dyed to give it a colour. A few washes later it starts to fade and the original begins to shine again.

KASHMIR

Warriors in Burqa

'There was such a madness for freedom that I believed that just by my taking up the gun we would achieve it.'

—*Ruhi*, member of the first organized group of women from the Kashmir Valley to go to a PoK camp for arms training

TRAGICALLY, TERRORISM AND KASHMIR HAVE BECOME synonyms. The graph of militancy for azadi or secession from the Union of India here, has over decades, had its share of spikes and dips but Kashmir has remained a simmering cauldron. New actors emerge every few years to continue stoking the fire, with Pakistan always the pivotal player. There was a spurt in homegrown militancy in late 2015 and early 2016. The icon of what is dubbed as 'new age militancy' was 22-year-old Burhan Muzaffar Wani, commander of the proscribed terrorist group, Hizbul Mujahideen (HM). Charismatic Burhan used social media, on which he was very popular, to amass a huge following amongst educated Kashmiri youth. College-going girls were reportedly his fans. His killing in an encounter with security forces on 8 July 2016 brought protests and unrest across the Valley, the like of which had not been seen since 2010. The 'Burhan aftermath' saw a large turnout for a women's-only protest rally in Tral led by female separatist leader Asiya Andrabi. In 2016, for the first time ever, schoolgirls abandoned their classes to pelt stones on security forces to resist them and allegedly provide cover to militants in hiding. Through 2017, street protests were on the rise as security forces intensified their hunt-and-kill operations against terrorists.

Natural beauty and man-created bloody violence co-exist in the Kashmir Valley in a most poignant way. Neither seems to sway the other. The chinar leaves turn amber each season. Nimble streams meander merrily through the villages, oblivious to the blood that at times mingles with the Jhelum waters. Lakes continue to be placid sheets of silver even when bloated dead bodies break their surface. Snowflakes hurriedly throw a blanket over unmarked graves and telltale blotches of red. Grazing sheep scamper when gunshots ring across rolling slopes only to return to munch contentedly on the fresh green blades of grass that appear on the cue from the weather gods. Rugged mountain passes look down unconcerned as harbingers of death carrying rifles under their phirans walk by. Golden haystacks stand innocently though they may hide lethal arms and ammunition. Shiny red apples weigh down branches concealing bullet-marked heads and slit throats. The perpetrators of violence in Kashmir, the Indian state nestling on its northern tip and sharing a border with Pakistan, have surely not been influenced by Kashmir's sublime beauty. Since the 1980s, Kashmir, the 'paradise on earth', as hailed by poets and Mughal kings, has provided the setting for a bloody insurgency and a militant secessionist movement that has brought under its arc young and old, men and women and even children. The incongruity of brutal killings in the backdrop of such overwhelming beauty has over the years come to be lost on its people.

Ruhi

The beauty of the Valley was lost, too, on sixteen-year-old Ruhi (name changed), when on a cold March evening in 1990, the schoolgirl stood with a group of six teenagers on the edge of Dal Lake, the 'Jewel of Srinagar'. The second-largest lake in the state of Jammu and Kashmir, the Dal in Srinagar, capital city of Kashmir, is more than its biggest tourist attraction. The locals use it as a waterway to travel to villages on its banks and connect to the road network. Ruhi had no eye for the pink lilies floating on the dark water, the reflection of the snowcapped Pir Panjal mountains in the lake or honeymooning couples wrapped in a romantic embrace in shikaras. Ruhi was involved in a different romance, the new romance that in the 1990s gripped the honeymoon destination, Srinagar. It was the romance of the gun. She could not wait to hold one in her hands.

The Jammu and Kashmir Liberation Front (JKLF) demanding secession from the Union of India was offering guns to the youth of Kashmir. Intelligence agencies had noted that in February of 1988 the first batch of boys had been sent to an arms training camp in PoK (Pakistan occupied Kashmir for India and Azad Kashmir for Pakistan). Two boys, Bilal Siddiqui and Maqbool Illahi of Srinagar, had crossed over via Kupwara, taking the Ration Pora-Dumari Gali route to enter Athmuqam in the Neelam valley of PoK for arms training.

Till then Kashmiri women, confined to family and home, had merely watched their men cross over to camps on the other side (PoK) for training. Their participation in the emerging militancy was limited to providing food and overnight shelter to militants from Pakistan as well as locals in their homes and protecting them from the security forces. The jury is still out on whether this was by choice or in the absence of one.

The JKLF's heady battle cry for azadi—freedom—turned the 90s into the romantic era of insurgency in Kashmir. While the men crossed over to PoK to train for a jihad, a holy war, to break free from Indian control, the women stepped onto the streets of the Valley, shedding the privacy of home decreed by their culture and tradition. Their overt participation in street protests marked a change in the role of women in the azadi movement. They now went public with their support of jihad in Kashmir. The passion of Kashmiri women for azadi was unabashedly on display in its main boulevard as well as in its narrow twisted by-lanes.

The organized large-scale moral support to sons, husbands and brothers who were taking up the gun for the freedom struggle was the first societally approved step by Kashmiri women to participate in the Pakistan-fuelled insurgency. Beginning in the late 80s and into the 90s, Kashmiri women gave moral strength to militants by their open embrace of them. The militant movement gained social legitimacy because the women publicly held mujahideens(freedom fighters) in high esteem. They lionized them in song and action. Funeral processions of the dead militants in the 90s were accompanied by hordes of women chanting 'As-salaam, as-salaam aye shahido, as-salaam, aaj teri maut pey ro raha hai yeh aasmaan.' (Greetings, O martyr, today the sky cries at your death).

They countered the police during protest marches by flinging red chilli powder in their eyes. Army and paramilitary convoys often encountered roads lined by women shouting 'Jeevey, jeevey Pakistan.' (Long live Pakistan).[1] This was a great propaganda tool for mujahideens and militant organizations who used it to enlist more men into their ranks. Often women in burqa would keep a watch on movements of the security forces and block their way as they zeroed in on terrorists hiding in congested localities. This would give time to the militants to make their escape down narrow staircases and alleys.

For the past year, Ruhi, like other young women, had abandoned her classroom to throng the streets and take part in protests. Sometimes it was to raise slogans against alleged atrocities by the Indian Army and at times to hinder search operations in congested residential areas by the police. In February 1989 Ruhi was part of the protest against Salman Rushdie's book, *Satanic Verses,* in Srinagar in which one person

1. Author's interviews with serving policemen.

was killed and 100 injured. She had escaped unhurt. No, she had not read the book but had been told it was an insult to Islam. Often she joined the women on the street to call out 'Mujahid jag zara, ab waqt-e-shahadat aaya hai!' (Wake up, holy fighters. It is time for martyrdom!). The killing of Ishfaq Majid, chief commander of the JKLF, in March 1990 in an encounter with security forces in Srinagar had brought a fresh upsurge of agitating teenagers.

Till early 1990, the gender role in the azadi movement was well defined in accordance with the code of conduct of a patriarchal society from which it had sprung. It did not permit frontline female militants. Transgression of this rule was unheard of. But it was sixteen-year-old Ruhi and four other girls who were to make a break from this tradition and push the boundaries of the role of women in the militant movement.

Ruhi and her friends had agreed to go for arms training to a camp in PoK. It was a landmark journey, not only for Ruhi personally but also for the history of women's participation in militancy in the Kashmir Valley. Ruhi being sent sarhad paar (across the border) for arms training to return as a trained JKLF militant to battle government security forces revealed that leaders of the militant azadi movement had changed their mind and decided to induct women as frontline combatants. Ruhi, along with four other girls, was to become a member of the first, and as it turned out, last known organized group of women from the Kashmir Valley to be smuggled across the border to a PoK camp for arms training.

Till now the militant wing of the JKLF, cashing in on the fact that women then were above suspicion of security personnel, were recruiting girls in the age group of seventeen to twenty-two years for a limited role. They were being used as couriers, to escort men and carry hidden arms from one place to another and gather intelligence on the movement of armed forces and locations of their bunkers. Some were being trained to motivate other women and schoolgirls to help the azadi war being waged by the men. They collected donations for the movement to finance jihad. A tall and lean youngster, Yasin Malik, had been declared president of the JKLF and was emerging as the idol of Kashmiri youth as an azadi crusder.

It was the thrill of meeting Yasin Malik that started the group of five girls on an ominous journey, the story of which Ruhi now wants to be made into a Bollywood film. 'Us zamaney mein to main heroine bhi ban sakti thi. Khubsoorat thi. Mujhe beauty queen ka khitab diya tha sab ne. Mera ghar kisko nahin pata tha.' (At that time I could even have been the heroine in the film. I was beautiful. Everyone called me the beauty queen of Srinagar. There were none who did not know where I lived). Boys hung around her house and on her way to the Nawakadal School of which she was the hockey champion too. If they got out of hand, Ruhi would swing her hockey stick menacingly to shoo them away.

*

Twenty-five years later it is not easy to locate Ruhi's house. It has taken me hours to find the locality she is known to be living in on the outskirts of Srinagar. Here no one wants to accept that they know her or are familiar with her name. Yet small chinks appear in curtains of houses where I have enquired about her and watchful eyes follow to see where I am headed. I finally call her mobile phone to say I am lost. A soft but eager voice urges me to continue down the road, instructing me not to ask for her. A few yards down the lane, a burly man steps out of a gaily painted gate to a double-storeyed house. He waves to me. As the gate is opened again a young woman dressed in a pink salwar kameez, her head covered with a shawl to partially conceal her face from view, holds out her hand to me in a gesture of welcome.

She is still beautiful. Her cheeks no longer have the flush of youth but time has had little success in completely erasing her classic Kashmiri good looks. The sharp aquiline nose, dark brown almond-shaped eyes, alabaster complexion, bow-shaped lips behind which peep pearly teeth give a fine account of why she was once hailed a beauty queen.

Her smile is bright but fails to reflect in her eyes. They hold a sad shadow. Even as she plays the gracious hostess, settling me down on the carpet, fussing over putting cushions behind me for comfort, I try to place who she reminds me of. She introduces the man as her husband and requests him for tea. Within minutes the famed Kashmiri dastarkhan is spread out on the cloth placed on the carpet. It is obvious that she has prepared for my visit. Then with a nod of her head she dismisses her husband before she starts to talk.

'Aap ne phirse zakham khol diye. Sab kuch phir se ankhon ke samne ghoom gaya...jaise kal hi hua tha.' (You have reopened the wound. Everything again has flashed before my eyes as if it happened only yesterday). Ruhi starts to sob. She cannot stop. She takes a deep breath and sighs. She tries to speak again. Her voice chokes. She takes the end of her pink-flowered chador and wipes away her tears. She makes another attempt to relate her story as she has agreed to. 'Maine bahut kuch saha hai... bahut dukh saha hai....itna saha hai ki meri zindagi par ek film ban sakti hai.' (I have borne a lot, a lot of pain, so much that a film could be made on my life). Then she slumps in resigned helplessness. Her hands fall to her side lifelessly. She closes her eyes as if trying to shut out the painful memory of her days of torture. Then she suddenly sits up and looks straight ahead into the distance. Her voice is determined. She shrugs as if to shake off the baggage of the past. Once again she decides not to let her past overtake her present. 'Chaliye, mein apni kahani sonaungi...zaroor bataungi jisme koi aur ladki woh galti na kare jo maine ki. Par meri ek shart hai. Mera naam nahi khulnaa chahiye na mera pata milna chahiye...mein sach se darti nahi hoon...darti hoon apne bachcho ki liyey...unki khushi na loot jayey meri kahani ke vajah se. Mere shouhar ko sab malum hai par bachcho ko nahi. Aap mujhko Ruhi naam de doh meri kahani ke liye.' (I will tell you my story, I will definitely relate it so that no other girl makes the mistake I made. But I have one condition. My name and address should not be revealed...I am not scared of the truth...I am only scared for my children... their happiness should not be compromised because of my story. My husband knows everything about me but not my children. You call me Ruhi for the story).

Then it hits me. Yes, Ruhi reminds me of Meena Kumari, the legendary tragedy queen of Indian cinema. Pain has lent a poetic lyrical beauty to her face, her bearing and her words which come together as a whole to dramatize her fateful life. I have missed it all this while because I have been searching for an adventurous, gritty person who decided to go on a journey no other girl in Kashmir ever had. Ruhi of 1990 was just that. But the fun-loving daredevil was lost in the eventful years that followed.

It was one of her school friends with whom Ruhi had bunked class and joined street protests who told her to join the struggle for azadi now that the anti-Rushdie agitation had petered out. If Ruhi wished she could become a full-time soldier in this fight for her watan (country). The friend said she knew Hamid Sheikh, the local JKLF commander who sent boys across the border to Azad Kashmir (as Pakistan and its supporters refer to PoK) for arms training to prepare them to fight the security forces of the Indian government. His name was as familiar to Ruhi as Yasin Malik's. A couple of months ago, in 1989, she was part of the mass uprising in Hamid's support triggered by his being wounded by a bullet in a clash with security forces. Ruhi, who had just finished with her Class 10 examinations, decided to volunteer. This would also give her the opportunity to meet Hamid Sheikh and Yasin Malik, who were spearheading the movement. 'Azadi ka aisa junoon tha ki humko lagta tha ki bus hamare bandook uthaane se hi azadi mil jayegi.' (There was such a madness for freedom that I believed that just by my taking up the gun we would achieve it).

The frenzy for azadi had numbed her every other emotion. All she could think of was her training which would help free Kashmir. It drowned her gratitude to her father who had ignored the disapproval of conservatives to support his daughter's unconventional wish to be a hockey player and train with the National Cadet Corps (NCC). Nor did she give a thought to her ever-loving indulgent mother. She told them nothing. Putting her sister-in-law under an oath of silence, Ruhi left with her friends for the 'sarhad paar' trip. I will be back after a month, Ruhi assured her bhabi.

On a March afternoon Ruhi, along with four of her classmates and the brother of one of them, left their homes in downtown Srinagar in an ambulance. A white van with an attention-grabbing cross painted in red on it and its wailing siren was their cover to drive undetected through the curfew-bound town. The police stopped them several times but they pretended to be taking an ailing relative to hospital. The ruse worked and soon Ruhi with her friends arrived at the Dal Lake. As she stood waiting for a shikara, she felt a rising excitement just as she always did at the start of a hockey match. Could the others hear her heart thumping as if trying to escape the constraints of her ribs? She had broken free of family and traditional societal ties. Now it was for her to free Kashmir. There was something romantic about wielding a gun, donning a uniform and finding a cause to stir passion. The risks and challenges ahead made it all the more alluring. The lurking daredevil in Ruhi had had enough of hockey tournaments, street protests and scaring away admiring neighbourhood Romeos. This was something far bigger. Ruhi was raring to go.

At the Dal Lake the group got into a waiting shikara. They sat in silence as daylight started to give way to evening. The falling dusk provided a cover for the wannabe militants. The shikara glided across the lake, the heart-shaped ends of its oars, the delight of honeymooners, silently slicing the darkening waters. Noise was the enemy of the moment. Ruhi was silent for reasons more than security. Dreams linked to the journey she had embarked on swirled in her mind like the concentric circles being made by the shikara oars as they caressed the Dal backwaters.

Late in the night the group disembarked at Point Hajan to wait for dawn. Next morning they were provided a car to drive to Sopore. From there they took a two-hour bus ride to a border point in Kupwara. Till now the going had been easy though the fear of being stopped and questioned by security forces was never far away. At Harnahama point, Ruhi's group was joined by twenty other boys under the JKLF banner. There were a number of batches from other organizations but none had girls. This did not bother Ruhi.

From here began the arduous part of the adventure, one that proved to be an endurance test for the physically fit Ruhi. For four days and four nights they climbed high mountains. Ruhi was surprised to see they had bunkers built into them where they rested a while. Then it was a descent into valleys, wading through waist-high snow. They nibbled at the biscuits and few rotis they were carrying. Water had to be rationed. Snow had seeped into her shoes. The blankets wrapped around her gave little warmth. Fatigue was setting in but she had come too far to return. Not that Ruhi thought of it even for a second. She just wanted the journey to end on the other side of the sarhad.

The wireless set in the hands of her group leader crackled. A tired but enthusiastic Ruhi heard him say over the wireless that the batch was ready for crossing over. She was filled with a sense of relief as she understood they had reached a crucial stage in the journey. As she stood in the snow she heard the instructions. Firing by security men guarding the Line of Control (LoC) that runs between India and Pakistan was going to begin soon. This was to be a cover for her and her companions to go across to PoK. The firing was to be only for a short duration and if they did not quicken pace they would be fired at. How am I going to run across snow, thought Ruhi. Before she could work it out she heard the sound of fire. As she lifted her foot to make a run she realized her toe had gone numb. There was no sensation and her foot dragged like dead weight. 'Bhago,' shouted the group leader, 'pul paar karo. Us paar Azad Kashmir tumhara intezaar kar raha hai.' (Run. Cross the bridge. On the other side Azad Kashmir awaits you).

Some 200 yards away hung a rope bridge. Ruhi's spirits soared when she sighted it. With a spurt of renewed energy she made a dash for it, dragging her foot as fast as she could. The sound of firing was already dying down. Ruhi did not care. She had crossed the swaying bridge and was no longer on Indian territory. They were now in Dhudniyal village in Azad Kashmir.

She grabbed the piping hot cup of tea offered to her as she crossed the bridge. People were waiting for them with tea, sweets, fresh clothes and blankets. The warm welcome was enough for Ruhi to forget her frostbitten toe, the hunger gnawing at her stomach or the discomfort of her now wet and dirty salwar kameez. The thrill of making it across the bridge compensated for all the pain and discomfort. Ruhi now looked forward to the promised training in handling guns which would free her side of Kashmir just like the part she had come to. Then she got her first shock.

Instead of being taken to a training camp the girls found themselves under virtual house arrest in a guesthouse in Muzaffarabad, many hours drive from the point of crossing. The boys who had come with them from India were taken to a factory building. To her utter dismay she saw that things were far from what had been promised by their recruiters back home. There were no clothes for them to change into. The rice given to them was infested with insects. Ruhi and her friends had pick to out the insects before they had their meal of the day.

The second shock for Ruhi was the complete transformation she saw in the JKLF leaders who had indoctrinated them and convinced them to sneak across the border to train in Azad Kashmir camps. They were now unapproachable and unwilling to hear their complaint of harassment at the hands of their trainers. The austere, ideologically charged, committed workers had changed to men of leisure, living a high life. They had not a thought nor time for the miserable living conditions of the ones who had undertaken a dangerous journey at their bidding.

The five men, wearing Pakistan Army uniforms, who stationed themselves at the guesthouse, introduced themselves as their trainers. Their arrival marked the beginning of a nightmare for the girls. As the trainers taught them how to use an assault rifle or pistol, their hands wandered all over their bodies. Initially the girls squirmed but it resulted in more brazen groping. Palms were pressed and held longer than required as the trainers taught them how to lob hand grenades. Religious sermons on the Islamic way of life were far too explicit for comfort when they talked about the duty of a woman towards her man in the marital bed and other ways of keeping him happy. The physical and mental stress was becoming unbearable for ideologically motivated Ruhi and her companions. They discussed it in whispers for fear of being heard by the trainers. Had they forsaken their homes and loved ones for this? The trade-off was not only a let-down but definitely not worthy of the sacrifice they had made.

One morning Ruhi awoke to find three of the girls missing. They had disappeared overnight. Fear gripped Ruhi. Where had the girls gone or had they been taken away? The answer she got made her go pale. Her fears multiplied. The girls have got married and gone off with their husbands, informed one of the trainers. The smirk on his face and the leer that curled his lips told her more than his words. Three of the other trainers had also disappeared. They were the same men who for the last two days had taken the now missing girls to isolated rooms on the pretext of 'special' training. 'Hum samajte thein kya ho raha hai. Un ladkiyon ki shakal ek kitab thi, sab likha tha' (We understood what was happening. The faces of the girls were like books in which everything was written). 'Hum apne khair ke dua kar rahe thein.' (We were praying for our safety). Was marrying the exploiter who forced himself on her the only respectable way out of this messs? Ruhi and the other girl left with her knew they were running out of time.

The escape was planned in a hurry. Ruhi and the other girl sneaked out of the window of their room after lights were switched off for the night. They started to trek towards Indian Kashmir. They knew the track and at night it was totally deserted. Still, they kept in the shadows. After a few hours they could see the outline of the rope bridge they had crossed to enter PoK. They now had to make a return dash, again in record time. Any movement on the bridge could be seen from a distance. As they left the cover of trees to run to the bridge hanging across a narrow span of flowing water, the men burst on them. They had been following the girls, keeping a safe distance, waiting to pounce on them at the right moment. The escape bid had failed when they were just a mile away from freedom.

Ruhi and her companion were hauled back to the military training camp. Things became worse. 'Ab hum unke dushman ban gaye thein.' (Now we had become their enemies). And that's how they were treated. Now there was no pretence of arms training. They were confined as prisoners in separate rooms. The trainer would drop in whenever he wished. 'Uske aane ko hum rok nahi sakte thein.' (We could not stop him), says Ruhi, her eyes now downcast. She holds up her hand as if pleading that I don't ask the obvious question. 'Aap bhi aurat hain aur mein bhi' (You are a woman and I am too), she says in an appeal for understanding and sparing her from detailing her humiliation.

*

'Write,' he ordered, thrusting a paper and pen in her hands. The man claimed he was from the ISI (Pakistan's Inter-Service Intelligence) and wanted her to write to her father informing him that she was fine and happy. Ruhi wrote the letter in Hindi, telling him she would be back soon. About thirty days after she had written the letter, one of her trainers brought it back to her and demanded that she decode the secret message she had sent in it. Taken aback, Ruhi said her letter could be shown to anyone of their choice who could read Hindi and they would know that it contained no secret message. No one believed her.

Her interrogation at the nearby gun factory turned out to be unbearable verbal and physical torture. Ruhi refuses to tell what they did. What she does want to disclose is her dismay at seeing Zaved Mir, the man who had indoctrinated her in Srinagar and on whose directive she had crossed the border, not come to her rescue. 'Woh toh sahib ki tarha reh raha tha aur mazey kar raha tha. Koi madat ke liye nahin tha.' (He was living like a sahib and enjoying himself. There was no one to help me). Ruhi soon realized that Mir, who was often there during her interrogation, was not keen to see her return either. There was no way out of the clutches of these men either in PoK or even back home in Srinagar.

The offer came a few days later. Her one-time trainer proposed marriage. Ruhi took no time in saying yes. You were not forced into marriage then, I ask in surprise. 'Iss nikah ke bare mein kya kahoon. Na meri marzi se tha na marze ke khilaaf. Mere liye yeh ek rasta tha aur bezaati se bachne ka.' (What can I say about this marriage. It was not with my will nor against it. For me it was a way to escape further humiliation). Ruhi reconciled herself to her fate. If she could not escape PoK, marriage to the trainer was her best option. Once married to him, she was allowed to leave the gun factory and set up house in town. She started to train as a nurse to look after the injured and sick at the local hospital. Soon Ruhi discovered she was pregnant.

Ruhi was ecstatic when her husband told her he was going to India for some official work and would contact her family in Srinagar. He promised he would take her to India on his next trip. She waited for his return for fifteen days. Was there to be another twist in her life? Ruhi decided to find out. She took out the paper on which she had noted a Lahore telephone number and address which he had once given her. Her friends from the hospital gave her some money and packed food and helped her board a bus to far-off Lahore, the second-largest metropolitan area in Pakistan and capital of Punjab province.

The man at the public phone booth at Lahore bus stand looked up in surprise at the number he had been asked by the woman to dial. It was the number of a well-known film studio and not that of a military office as the woman insisted. Ruhi begged him to make the call and ask for her husband's name. She recognized the voice when he came on the line. Overjoyed at hearing her husband's voice, she asked where his office was and how to get there. He told her to wait and he would soon come for her. When he arrived, Ruhi learnt who he really was. He was not from the army sent to give arms training. He was a 'jasoos' (spy). Ruhi couldn't really care either way. He was her husband. What he said next, however, made the world of a difference to Ruhi.

He told her that he had married her as part of his assignment. He had another wife. Ruhi did not burst into tears or freeze in shock. She quickly accepted what life was handing out to her and tried to make the best of it. She asked her husband to take her to his home. After all Islam allowed more than one wife and it was acceptable to her. What shocked Ruhi was his refusal to do so. She started to cry, pleading that he should not abandon her as she was seven months pregnant with his child.

Ruhi's husband had a solution. He told her he was going to take her home to India in a few days' time. Till then she was to stay with his friend's family in the Samnabad area. In a few days he got her a Pakistani passport. They crossed over to India at the Wagah border point. It was an excited Ruhi who boarded a train for Delhi with her husband from there. Though she had never been to Delhi, she felt she was going home. All that mattered was that she was back in India and would soon be on her way to Srinagar. Her husband told her that they would spend a day in Delhi and then make their way to Srinagar. When Ruhi got off the train at New Delhi's Nizamuddin railway station, she first wanted to call her home in Srinagar. But her husband told her to wait till they found lodgings in a guesthouse in Lajpat Nagar, a crowded locality in South Delhi with a busy marketplace.

With trembling hands, Ruhi held the lone telephone at the guesthouse reception desk. She was to speak to her family after almost a year and a half. But it seemed as if a lifetime had gone by. So much had happened from the day she had taken the shikaraat at the Dal Lake. Instead of hearing a familiar voice at the other end, a recorded voice informed her that the dialled number did not exist. She turned to her husband for help.

He was not there. She looked around thinking he may have stepped out to get food. He never returned. Ruhi had no money, nor any travel papers. Her Pakistani passport was also gone. She was frantic. All she had was a room for which her now missing husband had paid for two days. She stumbled to her room and felt the roof caving in on her. As the walls swirled and the floor heaved, she realized she was going into a faint. I can't allow myself to fall. I will hurt my child, Ruhi told herself.

It was the sound of the dialect of her home that made her open her eyes. She actually did not want to continue living and dealing with her unending misfortune. It was the voice of a stranger, a Kashmiri shawl seller who had run to hold the obviously pregnant woman as she was about to fall. He had recognized her as another Kashmiri. Ruhi requested him for help. She told him that her husband had abandoned her and she was unable to call home because she could not get through on the number she had. Could he help her send a letter to her father? The man said he could do more. He was flying to Srinagar later in the day and he would personally deliver it to the Srinagar address. He then brought her a loaf of bread to eat. Ruhi did not touch it. She sat on the bed and cried through the night. She did not know when she fell asleep.

Someone was trying to break open the door. Ruhi saw that it was daylight and someone was actually banging on her door. She opened the door. She collapsed in a heap at the sight of the man at the door. There stood her father in a crumpled salwar suit and bathroom slippers. She sobbed for forgiveness. Gently he lifted her up, held her hand and said,' Chalo, ghar chalo.' (Let us go home).

'Abbu ne kapre bhi nahi badle na jootey pehne. Jaise hi unko mera khat mila woh bhage Dilli ka jahaz pakadne ki liye.' (Father did not even change his clothes or wear his shoes. The moment he got my letter he rushed to catch a flight to Delhi).

Her homecoming brought the police to her father's door. The whole of Kashmir now knew of Ruhi, the girl who had returned from PoK after military training. The police wanted her. There were police raids on her house but her father and brothers hid her at various places. They did not want Ruhi to be taken away by the police when she was to have a baby soon. Ruhi could not bear to see her old father and brothers rounded up by the police and taken for interrogation about links with groups in PoK as well as recruiters in Kashmir. The day Ruhi saw red streaks across her father's back, she decided to give herself up to the police. Punish me for my mistakes but don't torture my father and brothers, she told them. She was often called for questioning. 'Mere saath jo hua tha meine bata diya. Jo kuch maloom tha bataya. Mere paas koi androoni khabar nahin thi.' (I told them all that had happened to me. Whatever information I had, I gave them. I told them that I had no inside information).

Ruhi's father and mother prayed she would have a safe delivery. They told her not to bother about people who would ask about the newborn's father. They decided the child would take her family name. When the child was born her father even gave a share of his property to the new family member. All he wanted was that Ruhi start life afresh. He urged her to start studying again. But it was not only the police and security forces who sought her out. She was in great demand by many separatist groups including the JKLF. Leaders from various outfits came to persuade her to join them. Some wanted to give her a leadership role. Some promised to give her arms as she had been trained to use a gun and pistol.

As the family sat around the dastarkhan every night for dinner Ruhi's father gave his counsel to them. Allah gives everyone a chance to make only one mistake. There is never room for another. Ruhi knew that the words were meant for her though he did not address her directly. She decided she would have nothing to do with separatist or political outfits. The only day her father advised her directly was when a letter arrived in her name. Her husband had sent divorce papers from Pakistan. Sign them and dispatch them by return post. Move on in life, he told her. When her child was six months old, Ruhi went back to her studies. Her parents urged her to join college, promising to take care of her baby.

*

The young man stepped out of his shop as Ruhi strode past. He did this every morning when Ruhi was on her way to college. She looked away and smiled to herself, basking in his obvious attention. Then she remembered her child at home and her past. Ruhi decided to change her route to college. The next day she saw him waiting at her college gate. He came up to Ruhi and introduced himself as a man in love with her. A flustered Ruhi requested a meeting to talk things over. Before she could finish speaking, he proposed.

This time Ruhi was in no hurry to accept. She told him all about herself and her child, adding it would not be right for a young bachelor to marry a woman with a past. What he said shocked her. Like everyone else he too knew that Ruhi had a child whose father was suspected to be a man at the PoK training camp she had run away to. Ruhi was devastated to hear that her story was not a secret. She was surprised that this man still wanted to marry her. She remained hesitant for some time. She put a condition. She would marry him only if his family approved and spoke to her father about it. Ruhi's father also had a condition. The nikah had to be a public affair followed by a registered court wedding.

At this juncture, her husband begs her to stop. He does not want Ruhi to tell her story. He is worried for her, for the family and for the life he has so painstakingly built for himself and Ruhi. He wants nothing to threaten it. But Ruhi does not want to stop. Does she not want to see her children educated and find a job that will bring them security, status and money? he asks her. This will jeopardize all this. What are you going to gain by telling all this, he asks? Ruhi seems not to hear him. He reaches out to hold her hand. Almost in a whisper, he pleads, Ruhi, please don't rake up your past for anyone. Forget it. She turns to me and says,'Mere shauhar farishta hai. Koi bhi ladki jisne meri tarah itni badi galti kari itni khush kismat nahi ho sakti ki mujh jaise shauhar miley.' (My husband is an angel. No girl who commits as big a mistake as I did can be so lucky as to get an angel of a husband as I have got). But today Ruhi is determined to continue. 'Mein aaj inki baat nahi manoongi. Meri kahani se aur ladkiyan shayad bach jayen.' (Today I will not listen to him. My story may save other girls). Sensing the build-up of tension between husband and wife, I offer to come again next morning. 'Kal shayad der ho jaya. Mere paas waqt hahin hai.' (Tomorrow may be too late. I am short of time).

Six months before we met, in September 2015, Ruhi had been told by doctors that she had stomach cancer.

A twist in her life once more?

*

The return of Ruhi in late 1991 brought instant death to the fervour of young girls wanting to go to PoK camps for training. Her story acted like icy water thrown on glowing embers. It extinguished the fire in them to go to any lengths for azadi. Ruhi's experience was not only sad but scary. It made them nervous. Ruhi's misadventure was discussed widely not only among the local mujahideen cadre but also amongst the large number of wannabe women militants. They withdrew from offering to turn armed combatants. Though young Kashmiri girls responded emotionally to the call for secession from India, the resistance movement's romantic era did not lead to the anticipated groundswell amongst women opting for training to be armed militants. They feared it would end up in their being exploited and taken advantage of. This was reinforced by another incident. Some three years after Ruhi's return, about 100 girls again took a chance in 1995 and crossed the border for arms training to PoK camp Darchies, Ilaqa-e-Ghair.[2] All of them disappeared, never to be heard of again.

From the looks of it, there was no place for women militants in separatist camps, very much in keeping with conservative Islam. Militant outfits operating in Kashmir do not grant equal

---

2. Author's interview in 2015 with former Hizbul Mujahideen militant, in Tanghdar, who trained in the same camp.

status to women. In their psyche, it is not for women to take up the gun. They believe Kashmiri women are nazuk (delicate) flowers easily crushed between one's fingers. While they could be used as facilitators, they could not be used as militants. In the PoK camps too the patriarchal mindset prevailed. The men saw the girls from Kashmir as objects primarily meant for their pleasure and not as jihadis who could fight shoulder to shoulder with men.

The majority of women in Kashmir realized this and accepted their limited role in the insurgency which did not require them to leave the security of their family and put themselves at the mercy of foreign militants. By now women were becoming increasingly essential to foreign militants not only to provide logistical support but also to display to Indian authorities their acceptance by the womenfolk and thereby give the azadi movement a veneer of a strong mass base. The reaction of the women of Machu on the outskirts of Srinagar in 1993, when a militant from PoK was gunned down by security forces, was one such display. Ismail, a militant from Pakistan, had been using a house in Machu for over three months to make telephone calls to his base across the border. The calls were being intercepted by security agencies and the spot was under watch. BSF (Border Security Force) men surrounded the house on a day they were sure of his presence there. He was shot dead as he tried to make his escape. As his body was laid out the women of the village gathered to wail. They not only embraced his dead body but smeared their foreheads and clothes with his blood to show ownership of the shaheed (martyr). Many women claimed he was a husband or a lover, and others that he was the father of their son.[3]

---

3. Author's interview with a BSF officer who took part in the encounter.

By 1993 the role of women had expanded from merely participating in street protests and as mujahideen facilitators. Women turned spies, mountain guides, honey traps and informers for militants. In 1992–93, militant organizations started to use beautiful girls to lure security men to lonely spots so they could shoot them dead. The girls were often paid for this, a price fixed according to the rank of the person they had brought in.[4] Such women usually ended up with a bullet through their heads or their throats slit.

In a significant development, women became important players in the separatist movement in Kashmir during that period not only for the militants but also the security agencies. Alleged exploitation of women, including sexual, by militants not only disillusioned the ones who had joined their ranks but made them turn to security forces to avenge abuse. For those engaged in anti-terror operations this was more than welcome. They too started to use women as informers, turning them into double agents often to be eliminated by one side or the other.

In 1993, two teenagers, Rafiqa and Sharifa, surrendered to the police. They told the police that they were fed up of being used for two years by militants to ferry arms from Baramulla to Srinagar at great personal risk. Information from them led to the arrest of several militants and recovery of two trucks of ammunition. They were provided protection and later slipped into the safety of anonymity.

The story of eighteen-year-old Daisy of Srinagar's downtown Zaina Kadal area did not have a 'happily ever after' end. Her death was tragic. She had arrived unexpectedly at the doorstep of a security forces office, drenched to the skin and sobbing uncontrollably.

---

4. Author's interview with senior army officer posted in Kashmir.

Daisy said that she had been kidnapped by five militants and confined to a houseboat on the waters of the Jhelum near Srinagar. Over five days she was repeatedly raped. When her tormentors were asleep, she had jumped into the water and escaped by swimming all the way to the security office. She wanted revenge. The distraught girl demanded a gun from the security men to return and kill her rapists. Acting on information provided by her, security forces swooped down on the houseboat and killed five militants, rounding up another twenty. Sadly, the government had no rehabilitation plan for Daisy. She was sent back to her parents. Two days later her body, hacked into three pieces, was found in the water near her father's carpet-weaving unit.[5]

It was a telephone call from a woman that led to the detection and arrest of a militant during the siege of a silk factory in the 1993 Nowhatta operation. The police had encircled the factory in which a militant was holed up. However a room-to-room search revealed nothing. The police control room received a call from a woman who refused to be identified but said she was witnessing the operation from her house. She informed them that the militant had made his escape and was posing as the driver of a parked fire brigade truck posted at the entrance of the factory. He was arrested following the tip-off.[6]

September 1995 saw a Kashmiri woman play a more daring and sinister role. Draped in a burqa, the woman walked into the Srinagar office of BBC/Reuters. She was carrying a parcel for correspondent Yusuf Jameel. As Mushtaq Ali, a photographer with Agence France Presse, opened the package,

5. Author's interview with retired senior police official, Srinagar, 2015.

6. Author's interview with police officer involved in the operation, Srinagar 2015.

it exploded. He was killed and two others injured.[7] It was an isolated case.

Militant organizations, till then mainly using women to facilitate their operations as informers, started to assign them other tasks crucial to take the azadi movement forward. Women were now asked to hide arms and ammunition in their homes, which were not raided by unsuspecting security men. The other task they were asked to undertake was to collect money from sources of militants. Since the men were under watch and often identified, they picked up ordinary women sympathizers and directed them to collect money from sources. The women, masquerading as shoppers or visitors to mazhaars and local fairs, went to pre-decided spots and carried back money handed to them by the contacts.

Observing all this, security forces no longer considered women to be above suspicion. They now saw them as a potential danger. In fact women operators became so relevant to agencies in anti-terror action in Kashmir that they coined a new generic term for them. 'Over Ground Workers' (OGW) is a common nomenclature in the files of the police and investigating agencies. OGW usually do not owe allegiance to a militant organization but to a jihadi brother, uncle or friend who is their 'handler'. They operate on the orders of the handler. OGW have yet to don a uniform and take part in frontline combat operations. There is only one rare photograph of a Kashmiri woman in combat attire holding a gun. The picture was recovered by the BSF after an operation on 29 August 2003 in Noor Bagh, Safa Kadal, Srinagar where Gazi Baba, chief commander of the Jaish-e-Mohammed, was killed. Gazi Baba was the brain behind the 1 October 2001 attack on the J&K State Assembly in Srinagar

7. UPI.com: journalists injured in Kashmir blast, 7 September 1995.

as well as the attack on Parliament House in New Delhi on 13 December 2001. The recovered photograph is understood to be of his wife, who discarded her army fatigues for ordinary clothes and managed to make her escape by calmly walking down the stairs while the operation was underway.

Logistical support provided by women to Kashmir militants was thus a well recognized fact by 1996. On 21 May 1996 at 6.30 in the evening, the Central Market in New Delhi's Lajpat Nagar was at its busiest when it was rocked by a blast. A car, later found to be a stolen one, laden with explosives, blew up in the South Delhi shopping hub, unleashing chaos and panic. The powerful explosion killed thirteen innocents and injured many others. The Jammu and Kashmir Islamic Front (JKIF) is said to have called up a media office in Delhi and taken responsibility for the bomb explosion. The blast, police suspected, had been masterminded by Bilal Ahmad, a Pakistan-based militant from Srinagar.

Farida Dar

One of the arrested suspects in the Lajpat Nagar bomb blast was Farida Dar, a Kashmiri woman from Srinagar. Though both Farida and Ruhi were fired by the same dream for azadi, they picked on totally different and opposite ways to fight the same war. Their choice not only reflected their personality but also what had come to be perceived those days as the best way for women to support the azadi movement. The fiery enthusiasm of Ruhi's times that had driven the naïve, young, impetuous girl to the battle frontline had given way to the likes of mature, cautious, worldy-wise, middle-aged Farida operating behind the scenes in a clandestine fashion. Farida Dar was a portly, bespectacled woman, popular as 'behenji' on account of being the sister of Bilal Ahmad, the locally revered jihadi living in Pakistan. Farida's younger brother, Bilal was in the first batch of boys who in 1989 crossed over to Pakistan to train to be a militant. He returned a month later and was arrested by the police. On his release, a couple of months before the 1996 Lajpat Nagar terror blast, he is learnt to have moved to Pakistan. Not only did the boys know that Farida kept in contact with Bilal but even intelligence agencies were aware of it.

Eight hours after the Lajpat Nagar bomb blast, the police was at Farida's house in Natipora, Dilsauz Colony, in Kashmir's Badgaon district on the outskirts of Srinagar city. The knock on her front door came when the dark of the night had not completely surrendered to the morning light. It was 3.00 a.m. The rattle on the door was loud and persistent. The police found it unusual that the men in the house did not come out to see why there was a ruckus at their doorstep at such an unearthly hour. Instead it was Farida, the lady of the house, who opened the front door. Was Farida expecting the police to come looking for her after the Lajpat Nagar terror incident, they speculated, as they later investigated the blast case. Who is in the house, they demanded to know. Farida declared that besides her, her husband, her parents-in-law and her son were the only ones there. The police stormed into the house to conduct a raid.

That was the beginning of Farida's tribulations. She was taken for interrogation to the Sher Garhi police station, suspected of being part of a conspiracy with other alleged active members of the JKIF to explode the bomb in Lajpat Nagar. She was taken to Delhi a few days later, on 24 May 1996. There was a non-bailable warrant of arrest against her. Farooq Khan, the then SSP (Operations) Srinagar, had informed Delhi Police that his reliable sources had provided clues to Farida being involved in the bomb blast conspiracy. Besides, the interrogation of an arrested JKIF man had implicated Farida.

One month later, on 7 June 1996, the afternoon sun beat down on the backyard of Farida's double-storeyed house. Farida was visiting her home after almost a month. Yet she had no difficulty in finding the spot under the pomegranate tree. She went inside the house and brought out a sharp metal object. Her face hidden by a burqa, and watched by women peeping out of the windows of her house, Farida started to dig. After about fifteen minutes she stopped. She had already dug two feet. With ease she pulled out a rexine bag. Inside the bag were two more polythene bags. Out of one of them, Farida took out two white slabs. Farida disclosed that the slabs were RDX. She opened the other polythene bag to reveal five timers weighing 1.325 kgs.

The police seized the unearthed explosives and timers and sealed them in a cloth bundle. A seizure memo was made according to the prescribed drill. Three days earlier in Delhi, while under police detention, Farida had disclosed details of the explosives she had hidden in her Srinagar home. She had led the Delhi police party to her house from the BSF camp where she had been kept in custody after being brought from Delhi by a police team. Farida could not explain when, from where and for what purpose she had acquired the explosives without any legal authority. According to the police, the RDX recovered from the green patch under the pomegranate tree in Farida's backyard was sufficient to blow up many buildings.

While the police had searched her Dilsauz house one month ago, when they had come to pick her up for interrogation hours after the Lajpat Nagar bomb explosion, they had not combed her backyard. The explosives and timers lay undetected under the pomegranate tree till Farida led the police to them. Judge S.P.

Garg, Patiala Court,[8] held that the prosecution had established that explosives and timers were recovered on the basis of Farida's disclosure statement[9] and she led the police to the spot where the stuff had been hidden. Farida was sentenced under Section 5 of the Explosive Substances Act of 1908 (punishment for making or possessing explosives under suspicious circumstances).

*

Fifteen years later, in September 2015, Farida denies everything. No, she did not hide any explosives or bury them in her garden. No, she had nothing to do with the Lajpat Nagar blast. No, she is not taking orders from her brother for any subversive activity. 'Of course I talk to him on the phone and have done so from the day he left for Pakistan. I want to know if he is fine and doing well. I talk only about his welfare. Which sister will not?' she asks as I try to break through her cautious reserve. Does she not know that her brother is a wanted man in India? What about the case against her and the court order? I persist. Her tone changes to that of one aggrieved. 'Jab ghar ke mard shaheed hotey hain ya arrest hotey hain to auraton ke liye museebat ati hai. Yeh kahani sab jageh ki hai.' (When the men of the house are martyred then their womenfolk have to suffer. This is the story everywhere). Farida's tone remains surprisingly level though the words are about her sufferings. For a moment we look at each other and she realizes I am looking for more. She throws up her hands as if her patience is running out and states, 'Police ne mujhse kaha ki woh mujhe chodh degi agar Bilal India wapas aa kar surrender kar de.' (The police told me that they would leave me alone if Bilal comes to India and

8. Sessions case No. 47/09 State vs Mrs Farida Dar @ Bahanji.

9. Disclosure statement Ex PW 39/A.

surrenders). Now that she has said her piece, obviously a well-rehearsed one by the sound of it, she is ready for the camera. She points to the camera in my hand and gestures that she will cover her face upto her eyes if I want to photograph her. As I am about to ask why, now that she is already sitting with men without a veil, she puts her finger to her lips and gestures towards the running tape recorder. I switch it off. Why does she have to cover her face for the photograph? I ask again. 'Yahan aisa hi karna padta hai' (here you have to do it), she replies. So short are her answers that there is just no space for any warmth to creep in while we talk. I feel she suspects me and is not convinced that I am meeting and talking to her only because I want to write about her.

There is suspicion in the air even as I stand on the doorstep of Farida's house waiting to see her. It is so tangible that I involuntarily look around to catch sight of who is watching me and from where. My query whether Farida is at home is met with silence. I tell the person who has answered the doorbell that I have an appointment. I can hear movement in the rooms behind. Someone comes out to inform me that Farida Behenji has gone out. I repeat that she has asked me to come at this hour. He disappears into the back of the house. Then another young man appears who starts an interrogation of sorts. Once again I tell him that I have spoken to her on the phone and explained the purpose of my visit and have come at a mutually agreed hour. He introduces himself as her son and wants to know the exact purpose of my wanting to meet with her. He goes back into the house and I am ushered into the formal sitting room. After a fifteen-minute wait, another man comes in holding a tray of soft drinks. This is the first sign of welcome.

Then Farida is escorted into the room by her son. He sits down protectively close to her. As I start a conversation I realize it is her son who wants to do all the speaking. And she is comfortable sitting in silence. I request that he let her speak for herself. The two exchange glances and he leans back, showing no signs of leaving her alone with me.

Her voice is calm, her expression deadpan. Farida displays no emotion as she recounts what happened on the early morning of 22 May 1996 when the police barged into her house and turned it upside down. After being in the house for an hour, she says the police told her that the search was over and she could shut the front door. But as she stepped out to do so, she was bundled into a waiting police jeep. According to Farida, she was driven to the Sher Garhi police post and was interrogated for twenty-four hours. 'They kept asking me over and over again where my brother Bilal Ahmad Baig was. I told them what I knew. My younger brother Bilal had crossed over (to Pakistan) with a batch of jihadis in 1989. He returned a month later and was arrested by the police. On his release in early 1996 he went to live in Pakistan.'

The police were apparently not convinced. 'They kept accusing me of being in contact with him and working at his bidding. Till then I had no idea of what had happened the evening before in Delhi at the Lajpat Nagar Market. I told them I did speak to him on the telephone now and then but it was only to enquire about his welfare.' It was on 25 May 1996, Farida says, that a Delhi police party of about fifteen arrived and took her by plane to the capital. From the airport she was taken to their Special Cell at Lodhi Colony and again grilled for information about her brother who they alleged was the mastermind of the Lajpat Nagar bomb blast. It was on 4 June 1996 that Farida made a disclosure to the police which led to the unearthing of explosive materials from her Srinagar house.

She recalls that Bilal was a young man of twenty years

when he first 'went across' leaving behind a letter for the family. 'The letter said he was going with a group of jihadis and would return after fifteen days. We were worried sick. I missed him. After a month my mother saw him at Lal Chowk, sitting in an autorickshaw. We waited for him to come home that evening. He came home only the next day. He had a watch repair business. But he was arrested and released after seven years and he immediately went to Azad Kashmir. I met Bilal for the first time after his going away only in 2002 when I visited Rawalpindi in Pakistan after my release from Tihar Jail. He came to the airport to see me. We had so much to talk about. He knew mere upar kya zulm hua uske wajah se (he knew what I had had to suffer on account of him). But I did not discuss this with him.'

Farida refuses to call her brother a wanted man or a militant. He is a jihadi working for a cause dear to him. And what about her? She refuses to give a straight answer. Farida's voice keeps to its monotonous tone as she says that even as a child she could not understand why her relatives lived in two countries instead of one. She recalls asking her father why her uncle could not come to India and they not go to Pakistan where he now lived. After all, we are one family, isn't it? It comes out more as a statement than a question. Her son now finds it difficult to restrain himself and takes over. All this India and Pakistan is a political game. We are all one and should be allowed to live in peace, he says. Are you not happy here in this huge house so well located in beautiful Kashmir? I ask. He takes my question as an accusation of sorts. 'Why should we not have a big house? We are not poor nor do we get money from Pakistan as Indian security agencies allege. My father has a flourishing watch repair business and we earn well.' Can I meet his father, Farida's husband? 'He does not like to meet people who ask too many questions. In fact, my mother too does not like to answer questions,' he says in a voice turning aggressive and signalling that I better be on my way.

Farida has listened to her son and decides to speak up. 'Yahan sab kuch theek nahi hai. Kashmir mein zulum hai. Bete ghar nahi wapas lauthe hain...gayab ho jatey hain. Ma rothi raha jati hain.' (Here, nothing is all right. There is a lot of suffering in Kashmir. Sons leave the home and do not return... they disappear. Their mothers keep crying). This is Farida, the social activist speaking. After living through a fourteen-year-long trial and spending four years in custody, Farida decided to become a social activist. On her release from prison, Farida was contacted by many separatist groups. They wanted her to join and take up a leadership role. She was made chief of the Jammu and Kashmir Liberation Council. But the identity she wants is of a person who is helping to find missing children and not that of a separatist leader. This she feels keeps her safe from security forces while giving her acceptability amongst her people. Given her past record, she knows she is on the watch list of intelligence agencies and is aware that it is wise to be careful and cautious. She has an organization of about 150 women trying to find their missing children. 'They have disappeared...picked up by the armed forces or police...we don't know.' Farida wears her hostility towards Indian security forces and mistrust of them on her sleeve almost as a tactic to establish her credentials as a true separatist sympathizer. It brings her a following amongst the people of Kashmir and, more importantly, recognition by political activist as well as separatist leaders there, and a place at their table. For Farida, being a human rights activist in Kashmir is less dangerous, if not less useful, than being a terrorist facilitator.

It was a year since the bomb blast in New Delhi's Lajpat

Nagar. But the news of the terror strike by Kashmiri separatists had caused no ripples in the life of people living in remote villages of the Kashmir valley. Their brush with militants was only when they came into their settlements looking for safe houses.

Nighat

A visit from militants was usually an unwelcome intrusion, like the one that turned fifteen-year-old Nighat's life upside down and sucked her into the dangerous world of Kashmir militants. It was 8.30 p.m. in 1997 in a village in south Kashmir and Nighat (name changed) had just lit the lamps. Her father had secured the doors and windows of their house, not so much to keep out the cold as to deter the bands of armed men who came often to their village in search of shelter and food.

There was a rattle on the door. Not too loud but firm and insistent. It was the dreaded knock. Nighat looked up apprehensively from the schoolbooks she had just started to work on. Her father gestured to her and his wife to withdraw into the rear room. He got up slowly from his perch on the carpet between two cushions and with a resigned look opened the door.

He stood tall, fair and handsome, his long hair brushing his shoulders. His penetrating honey-coloured eyes swept the room. He then turned a casual glance on Nighat sitting with her books. She refused to lower her gaze. She stared back defiantly at the thirty-year-old armed man. It was hate at first sight. He was a killer of innocent men. Though she had not seen him before, like everyone in the area she knew of him. The uninvited visitor was none other than the dreaded Khalid (name changed), the south Kashmir district chief of the militant outfit, Hizbul Mujahideen, since 1991. She detested his name even before she had seen him for he had spread terror and intimidated people.

The man at the door with his four armed companions demanded food and shelter for the night. Nighat saw submission in her father. He had shrunk into his phiran, lowered his eyes and his voice held no protest. Go and prepare a meal, he told his daughter. To everyone's surprise, Nighat refused. Why do we have to feed men who kill, she questioned as only a rebellious teenager can. Taken aback, Khalid slowly turned towards her. This chit of a girl had some guts, he thought. 'Aap ka naam kya hai.' (Whats your name)? he asked her directly. She gave it reluctantly. Why does your daughter hate me, he asked her scared father? 'Kyonki tum zulum kartey ho, logon ko maar daltey ho' (because you heap atrocities on people and you kill), Night spat out. Her father's order to keep quiet and leave the room put an end to the brief exchange between Nighat and the feared guest.

Nighat was asleep when the men left next morning. The militants always moved before the sun began to strip the shadows that provided them cover. Five days later they were back. Nighat started to talk to Khalid. Over a couple of visits the conversation changed course from the impersonal 'pass the salt' to a more personal quest to know each other. Nighat had many questions. Khalid was content just watching her dancing eyes and marvelling at her fearless way of conducting herself. There was not a person in her village or area who liked to cross his path, leave alone chat him up. Nighat was different. Not only was she not intimidated by him but apparently wanted to get to know him as a person. She asked him leading questions about his way of life, which according to her understanding entailed killing innocents. By the fourth visit Khalid had convinced Nighat that he had never killed anyone with his own hands.

His voice was surprisingly soft and his manners revealed a lovable nature...at least to Nighat. The young girl was taken up by the sadness in his voice when he spoke about encounters in which his men killed or injured people. This is not the sort of man who can kill, she felt. He does not behave like a militant. Nighat wanted to convince herself that Khalid was not a killer so she repeatedly asked if he had ever taken anyone's life. The answer was always no. She questioned him closely about his tasks as the chief of the local militant outfit. Khalid kept nothing back, enjoying the growing intimacy between them. One night she saw him distribute wads of currency notes to his men. He kept nothing for himself nor sent anything for his family. What an honest man, she thought. The more she met him, the more she was convinced that Khalid was actually trapped in the life of a militant.

Nighat was in love with Khalid. Falling for a jihadi was nothing unusual in the Kashmir of those years. Young girls dreamt of marrying mujahids. A jihadi had the approval of mothers as well. They spoke proudly of martyred sons. A song then composed, 'Kalashnikov lagai balayai, yenav ladayat path fairaleh' (I shower my life on this Kalashnikov, don't give up this fight for freedom) reflected the sentiment of the times. Damsels coquettishly sang 'Main mujahidov behan, Praraie hideout as' (O my beloved mujahid, I will wait for you at the hideout).[10] Instead of frowning at this brazen invitation, the conservative village society gave tacit permission to young girls to act on the ditty.

---

10. Manisha Sobbhrajani, 'Women's Role in Post 1989 Insurgency', *Faultlines: Vol 19*, April 2008.

Khalid and Nighat started to meet secretly. Whenever Khalid was in the area he would send word to her. Cooking up an excuse, Nighat would go for an evening rendezvous in secluded spots outside the village. They had to keep their affair a secret from the locals and also from the militants for the sake of their security. Khalid feared that if his love for Nighat became common knowledge, she would be hounded by security forces as they went about trying to nab him. Also, his leaders may ask him to pressure her to become a facilitator for the militants. The teenager and the thirty-year-old feared HM district chief were now deeply in love and could not help but meet at least twice a month. The conversation at their brief meetings often turned to Khalid's young wife and old father being hounded and tortured by security forces for information on him. His seventeen-year-old nephew had been picked up by them, never to return. Nighat started to fear for the life of the man she had come to love. She vowed to do whatever it took to keep him safe.

Like many other girls involved with mujahids in those days, she too started to work for her militant lover. She arranged safe hideouts for him, gathered information about the movement of security forces in the area, helped carry messages from him to his comrades, hid pistols and grenades under her burqa to deposit them at pre-arranged spots. Sometimes she pulled a veil over her face to escort HM cadres past security checks. Nighat became Khalid's partner in more ways than one. Now they were both living dangerously and Nighat was fully aware of it. As far as she was concerned, she was doing all this for love of Khalid. But for the security forces she was now as much of a dangerous outlaw as Khalid because she was assisting, facilitating, abetting and harbouring a terrorist. These actions come under the ambit of terrorist activity and such a person can be charged under various provisions of statutes dealing with terrorists.

Why endanger your life? Nighat would often ask Khalid. Each time she met him, she tried to convince him to surrender and come over-ground. All you have left is your life. Your home has been burnt down, your family is constantly harassed by the police for information about your whereabouts, she would point out. Give up this life. Not only did she love him, but she felt he was basically an honest and innocent man who would sooner than later be killed in an encounter with security forces. After many meetings and much pleading she started to feel that he would listen to her and surrender. 'Baki, maine Allah pe chod diya.' (The rest I left to Allah).

Nighat had known Khalid for six months when in 1998 she took the biggest risk of her life. As planned some fifteen days before, she left home on some pretext, travelled 20 kms by bus and arrived at the house of one of Khalid's comrades who was expecting her. It was Nighat's wedding day. But there was a hitch. No one had arranged for a cleric to perform the ceremony. Pre-arranging it could have led to a security lapse and Khalid's capture.

The militants knew well the power of their guns. Khalid's men barged into a wedding venue in a nearby village and forcibly carried the maulvi from there to a waiting Nighat. But the groom was still missing. It was a nervous bride who waited for his arrival. Cold shivers shook her body as her mind grappled with questions. Had the police apprehended him on the way? Had he been shot dead? Had her parents realized she had run away to marry a militant and were on their way to take her back? When Khalid finally arrived, it was without any fanfare. He just slipped in alone. The wedding ceremony had to be hurried through. To stay in one spot for too long would be a security breach for him. Nighat was beginning to realize what life with a militant was going to be like. She knew from now on she too would be on the run, constantly watching over her shoulder. This is not the life I want with Khalid, decided Nighat, as the maulvi approached her to seek her acceptance of Khalid as a husband.

The maulvi, in keeping with custom, asked Nighat for her assent to marry Khalid. Yes, she said, but added a condition. If the marriage had to be solemnized, Khalid would have to promise to surrender soon. The maulvi carried back the message to the waiting groom. Khalid did not hesitate. He said yes and the nikah was completed. Nighat could not ask Khalid about his promise to her when she was allowed to meet her husband after the ceremony. There was no time. They could not afford to stay in the same place for too long. But she knew that Khalid would keep his word.

The newlyweds had to part right away. Nighat returned to her parents' home and Khalid went away to hide in an undisclosed destination. Nighat was expecting her parents to fly into a rage when she broke the news of her marriage to Khalid. But she had not expected to be beaten for it. Her mother and brothers beat her black and blue. He will not be able to live long. He will be hunted down and you will be a widow in no time, they shouted as they rained blows on her. Over two days they tried to make her understand the foolishness of what she had done. You will always be on the run if you live with him, they warned. But Nighat had made her choice and there was no coming out of the marriage as her parents advised.

Two days later, she left her home for good and went to Khalid's sister's house to wait for her husband. She had no idea when she would see him as Khalid rarely came there, knowing the place was under police watch. It was a month-long wait before he arrived. Nighat the bride had only one request to make to her new husband. Please surrender and come over-ground so that we can lead a normal life, she urged. Where will I go if you are killed, she asked, breaking into tears. Her parents had shut their doors on her. Now she had only him and no one else. He told his teenage wife to plan his surrender. His only word of caution was secrecy. If the leaders of his outfit or any member got wind of it, he would be eliminated in no time. Then he vanished.

Nighat's first move was to contact a local politician who was her relative. But he was scared to take any action fearing retaliation from the militants. Nighat used all her persuasive skills and finally won him over. He in turn contacted Farooq Khan, the then head of the Special Task Force set up to track down militants. The feedback was chilling. Khalid was already on their radar. In a month they would have him in their net. That was the time he had left to live. Nighat was now desperate. She decided to meet Khan and beg for her husband's life. Word was sent to the Special Task Force chief. A car was arranged to take her to Khan's office. To hide her face Nighat donned a burqa when she went to meet Khan. As she drove to his office, she wondered what would happen if things did not go the way she hoped. They could well detain her. The other possibility was that the HM people would discover who Khalid's new wife was and that she was in contact with security forces. But Nighat decided to take the risk.

This was the first of several meetings over a month. Khan and Nighat were suspicious of each other. Khan had to convince himself that Nighat was not laying a trap. Nighat, on the other hand, wondered if Khan was trying to trap Khalid and then kill him. Again she decided to take a risk. She decided that Khalid and Khan should meet. Finally in 1999, it was arranged that a car be sent to pick up Khalid from a pre-decided spot. Nighat had the plan conveyed to her husband who was in hiding in a place even she did not know of. The secret meeting was on. All Nighat could do now was wait.

It was not an easy night. Nighat was all nerves. Would the meeting end in Khalid being killed in a false encounter? Would her husband surrender or back out at the last minute? Would his organization men find out about his plan and eliminate him before he met Khan? The questions kept her awake the whole night. Next day she could contain herself no more. She went to her politician relative to find out what had happened. She heard the news and collapsed on the floor.

A distant voice was telling her that Khalid had surrendered. Actually it was someone in the room giving her the news. Nighat had passed out on hearing that Khalid was safe and under the protection of the Task Force. The relief and release of tension at the news had made her dizzy. It was three days later that Nighat was allowed to meet Khalid.

Khalid was one of the biggest catches for the Task Force. He also turned out to be of great use later in nabbing an LeT divisional chief and the unearthing of a plot to disturb that year's Amarnath Yatra. The militant, understood to be on a recce, was spotted and recognized by Khalid in the marketplace. He tipped off the Task Force and gave his location. His arrest led to recovery of arms as well. However, he opened fire and was killed by the Force. But Khalid kept the promise Nighat had elicited from Khan before his surrender. She had asked that Khalid never be used to kill his ex-mates in any HM encounter.

*

Like always, Nighat is late. She may even not turn up. I wait anxiously for her to arrive. We always meet at a different place, the spot disclosed to me only half an hour before. The security drill she has imposed on herself is going to be followed more strictly for this meeting because Nighat has promised to bring her husband along. If there is the slightest hint of being detected or followed by HM men, she will abandon plans for the meeting. She has told me earlier that her plans are never firm because her life now has turned into a game of hide-and-seek that keeps her nerves on edge. Militants from HM have sent a message to her husband's ancestral home. They will kill Khalid whenever they spot him. Even fifteen years after his surrender they are hounding him. She has to watch her every step. The militants are looking for her because she can lead them to Khalid.

The burqa-clad figure enters the room unobtrusively. She looks around and chooses a chair away from the window and door. Nighat is reluctant to remove her veil. You can trust everyone here, assures the person in whose house we are meeting this time. As she uncovers her face it is easy to detect that the one-time unafraid teenager is now a thirty-year-old mother, full of fear and trepidation. Gone is the brave bearing that had struck hardcore militant Khalid. Her kohl-rimmed eyes dart from door to door, window to window, alert for any lurking danger. Her personality may be scarred by the life she is leading but the beauty that captured Khalid remains.

Khalid, walking a few paces behind, is also still drop-dead handsome. Life has been tough on him but it is easy to see why he made schoolgirl Nighat swoon and risk her future for him. He too has lost his swagger and his eyes are now filled with despair. His voice is that of a man disillusioned. Nighat takes the blame for it all. 'Maine zid ki aur surrender karaya. Par kabhi araam ki zindagi guzaarhi nahin.' (I insisted on his surrender but never have I lived a relaxed life). Khalid adds, 'Isse acchhi woh zindagi thi...maro ya maaro.' (Better than this life was the other one...either kill or get killed). But there can be no going back for Nighat and Khalid.

Nighat admits that life after Khalid's surrender has not turned out as she had imagined. But she is grateful that Khalid is alive and they can live together. She says she is proud that she could convince him to give up the life of a militant. Women in Kashmir are usually known for abetting militants either out of fear of them or out of sympathy for them but they also have the strength to convince them to give up arms, she says to me.

The government's indifference to surrendered militants is a reason for women not playing a role in convincing their men to come over-ground. After Khalid surrendered he was appointed an SPO (Special Police Officer). But it was a brief stint. According to her, his 'utility' ran out when he no longer had actionable information. Nighat and Khalid had to move from place to place for security reasons. He started a small business of readymade garments but had to shut it down and soon move to another town. There he ran a taxi but it caught fire. Money was running out. Though Khalid had surrendered with his AK-47 gun, the government did not give him the promised compensation for it.

Nighat went back to her studies so that she could get a job. But nothing appears to be working in their favour. Khalid cannot get a passport or a character certificate to get a job. Though Nighat has not been a militant, she has to keep a low profile to keep her husband safe. We are like untouchables. The government has no use for us anymore. No one wants to support a surrendered militant, be it political parties or government because of fear of militant organizations, she says, her voice heavy with sadness. 'Surrendered militant ke marne pe to koi rone ya gum zataney bhi nahi ata. Koi aurat apne bhai ya shauhar ko surrender karney par majboor kyo karegi. Woh toh usko madat karegi police se bachney ke liye...woh darke toh nahin jiyega. Government yeh nahi sochti hai. Hum to Allah ki meharbani se zinda hain.' (No one comes to mourn the death of a surrendered militant. Why would a woman persuade her brother or husband to surrender? Instead she will help him and save him from the police. The government does not give this a thought. We are alive by the grace of the Almighty). Does she regret getting involved with a miltant in the first place? 'Mein toh bus inke zindagi ki dua mangti rehti hoon. Maine socha tha inse surrender kara ke humey ek nai zindagi milegi. Jab mein Khalid ke saath gayee mera iss jihad aur azadi ki jung se koi lena dena nahin tha. Mein bus school jatee aur ghar rehti. Unka dar jaroor tha.' (I only keep praying for his life. I had thought that by getting him to surrender we would get a new life. When I decided to go with Khalid I had nothing to do with this jihad or battle for azadi. All I did was go to school and later stay at home. Yes, we did fear the militants).

Anjum Zamarud Habib

Nighat, the innocent village teenager, had little inkling about the sinister goings-on in the rest of insurgency-inflicted Kashmir. But miles away Anjum Zamarud Habib already had a role in it.

Anjum Zamarud Habib was no stranger to being apprehended by the police. As a young girl she was first picked up in March 1990 in Anantnag (Kashmir) during a crackdown by security forces to round up sympathizers and supporters of the azadi movement. But thirteen years later, Zamarud's arrest was a defining moment for her. Not only did it change her life but also highlighted the use of women by banned separatist outfits in Kashmir to move and collect funds for them.

On 6 February 2003, at 1.15 p.m., the taxi in which Zamarud was travelling in New Delhi screeched to a sudden halt. The car tailing it from the Pakistan High Commission in Chanakyapuri, the elite diplomatic quarter in New Delhi, had abruptly swung in and intercepted Zamarud's cab. Driver Narender Singh, who had been moving towards the Yashwant Place shopping complex and was at the crossing of Niti Marg and Satya Marg on the Nehru Park side, barely a kilometre from the blue-domed Pakistan High Commission, had no choice but to slam the brakes. Within a second the taxi was surrounded by a police team. Zamarud took in the fact that there was a woman inspector too. She felt the bile rise in her throat and she swallowed hard. Maybe it is only a routine check, she told herself by way of calming her nerves. Inspector Gurcharan Singh flashed his identity card and addressed Zamarud sitting motionless in the back seat.

'I am Anjum Zamarud Habib, daughter of Habibullah Bhatt, resident of House No. 830, Mohallah Mehman, Rishi Bazar, Anant Nag, Jammu and Kashmir,' said the forty-year-old on being asked to disclose her identity. The inspector informed her that a search was to be conducted. Initially Zamarud resisted but soon gave in. Woman Inspector Dhara Mishra moved in to search a black leather bag on the seat beside Zamarud as well as her purse. According to the police seizure memo also signed by Zamarud, the leather bag was stuffed with thirty bundles of hundred-rupee notes, each package of Rs 10,000 with slips affixed on them(totalling Rs 300,000). Her purse held Rs 7,000, her personal diary of 1997 with the names of banned terrorist outfits like Lashkar-e-Taiba, Jaish-e-Mohammed, Hizbul Mujahideen and Al Umar on pages dated 7, 8, 9 and 10 April with amounts against them, a Srinagar/Delhi/Srinagar Indian Airlines ticket, photo negatives, photos, Zamarud's election card, medicines, a silver ring and a pair of gold earrings.

Zamarud was arrested. As she was being taken to the Special Cell of the Delhi Police at Lodhi Colony, Zamarud felt that the foreboding she had when she arrived at the Pakistan High Commission earlier at 11 a.m. was playing itself out. Dread had overcome her as she had stepped out of the taxi. She felt as though an impending storm was brewing around her.[11] Onlookers saw no sign of fear on Zamarud's face as she walked straight in through the high commission gate, clutching a black purse in her hand. She came out at 1.10 p.m. carrying a black leather bag on her right shoulder and her purse in her left hand.

By then Narender Singh had responded to a call at 12.30 from the Pakistan High Commission to his taxi stand for a cab. Zamarud got into his taxi. Narender Singh recalled she was carrying one black leather bag and asked to be dropped at Malviya Nagar. But the taxi had barely driven 200 yards when it was intercepted by Inspector Gurcharan Singh. Unknown to Zamarud, a police team had been lying in wait for her on the instructions of Assistant Commissoner of Police L.N. Rao. The police officer had received definite intelligence at 9.30 that morning that a lady from J&K would visit the Pakistan High Commission at 11 a.m. to receive money to promote terrorism in India.

Inspector Gurcharan Singh reached the high commission with an informer at 12.15 p.m. The policemen on watch informed that a lady had come in a taxi at 11 a.m. and gone inside the building. As Zamarud came out of the high commission building and waited for a taxi, she was identified by the informer as the lady expected to collect the money from someone in the high commission. The police team was soon on her trail and swooped down on her within five minutes of her leaving the building.

---

11. Anjum Zamarud Habib, *Prisoner No. 100: An Account of My Days and Nights in an Indian Prison*, p. 3, Zubaan, New Delhi, 2011.

Revelations by Zamarud led not only to her arrest but triggered diplomatic action, bringing about a landmark dip in India–Pakistan bilateral relations during that era. Zamarud revealed that the three lakh rupees recovered from the black leather bag had been given to her by Pakistan Charge d'Affairs and then Acting High Commissioner Jalil Abbas Jilani to be taken to Srinagar and delivered to terrorist outfits mentioned in her seized diary. She said she had been instructed to go to the Pakistan High Commission by Abdul Ghani Bhat, the then chairman of the All Party Hurriyat Conference, and meet Jilani. A day later Zamarud confirmed before a Special Judge that she had received three lakh rupees at the Pakistan High Commission as 'nazarana' for Bhat.

Zamarud's disclosure statement also led to the arrest of Shabir Ahmed Dar of the Kashmir Awareness Bureau who she said had also received money from Jilani to promote terrorist activity in India. The police named Jilani in the FIR filed against Zamarud and Shabir. Two days later (8 February 2003) India expelled Jalil Abbas Jilani and four other staff members of the Pakistan High Commission. Jilani was asked to leave the country within forty-eight hours. The then spokesperson of the Ministry of External Affairs, Navtej Sarna, said in a statement, that 'we have hard evidence of what Jilani was doing, which was incompatible with diplomatic norms'.

On 14 February 2003, almost a week after her arrest near the high commission, Zamarud was lodged in Tihar Central Jail, Number 6, Delhi. Her confessional statement was recorded by the Deputy Commissioner of Police, Special Branch, in front of a magistrate and she was produced in a Special Court. After a week in Tihar Jail, Zamarud sent a letter dated 19 February 2003, retracting her confessional statement, stating that it was made under threat and claimed she had been falsely implicated.

According to Zamarud's letter, she had come to Delhi to obtain a visa for Pakistan and Bangkok to attend an international women's conference in Thailand. She was required to visit Pakistan to co-ordinate with womens' rights activists there. She had brought Rs 3,50,000 from Srinagar to buy computers for her voluntary womens' organization as well as tickets for her travel. She had visited the Pakistan High Commission on 6 February 2003, to collect a visa form. She further claimed that she was whisked away by the police when she returned from the high commission to the Malviya Nagar office of the Kashmir Awareness Bureau run by the Hurriyat where she was staying. She was asked by the police to be a witness against Hurriyat leaders and Pakistan High Commission officials. Since she refused, she was falsely implicated in the case. Zamarud not only alleged torture during police custody at the Special Cell at Lodhi Road but also said that she was made to write in the blank pages of her diary under threat of being paraded naked. She accused a woman police inspector of disrobing her and threatening to circulate her naked pictures.

On 7 August 2003, Zamarud was charged under Section 22(2) and 22(3) of POTA (Prevention of Terrorism Act 2002). For four years and seven months, Anjum Zamarud remained in Tihar as an undertrial, shunned and abused by fellow prisoners as a Kashmiri terrorist.[12]

The Patiala House court was milling with people on 28 September 2007 but Zamarud felt lonely and forlorn. 'Guilty' pronounced the designated POTA judge. Her head swirled as she heard a five-year rigorous imprisonment sentence handed out to her. The order read '...the prosecution has proved beyond doubt

12. Zamarud's letter to the National Human Rights Commission, dated 8 June 2007.

the accused, who was working for the liberation of Kashmir had collected Rs three lakhs from Pakistan High Commission to distribute to different banned terrorist organizations and therefore she committed an offence punishable U/s 22 (2) POTA. Hence she is convicted U/s 22(2) POTA'. Persons convicted under this section of POTA have received money or other property to use for the purposes of terrorism. Zamarud became prisoner No. 100 (Tihar Jail).

On 8 December 2007, she was released on bail by the High Court as she had already served the better part of her sentence behind bars. Anjum Zamarud felt her legs give way as she stepped out of the Tihar Jail gate at about 7.30 in the evening. In a daze she got into her brother's waiting car. Suddenly the world outside the Tihar Jail walls seemed strange to her. In her five years of incarceration, she felt she had forgotton to breathe and walk in vast open spaces. It made her dizzy. She asked the driver to stop after going a short distance. On her brother's suggestion, Zamarud stepped out of the car and took in gulps of fresh air. 'Look at the sky, stars, and moon,' he said, handing his mobile phone to her. 'Speak to our mother Boba. She is waiting in Srinagar to welcome you home.' But Zamarud felt nothing. She was bereft of emotion.[13] After almost five years in Tihar, Zamarud felt she was a wreck of a person.

*

Eight years later, Anjum Zamarud Habib is no longer the woman who was received by her brother Dr Hamidullah Bhat at the gate of Tihar Jail. It is a confident, purposeful-looking Zamarud who embraces me in greeting at her home. I search her face for the wounds and scars of trauma inflicted by a prison stay, so

---

13. *Prisoner No. 100*, p. 217.

vividly described by her in her book. There is no apparent trace of it. However a mere mention of her jail stint and her face clouds. She lowers her eyes and her voice is steeped not only in the pain she associates with it but also with bitterness. Why is she bitter? 'Women are often betrayed,' she says with some sadness but refuses to elaborate. You are too strong a woman to bother about betrayal, I say to cajole her to tell me more.

When she speaks again it is a barely audible whisper. 'The Hurriyat did not work for my release with the government as it had done for many others.' To her dismay she had learnt that her name was not in the list of Kashmiri prisoners her organization had submitted to the Indian government recommending release from jail.[14] On the other hand, proceedings against her co-accused, Shabir Ahmed Dar of the Kashmir Awareness Bureau, were dropped and he was released on 11 May 2004. 'I told my mother never to go to Hurriyat's doorstep to seek help. The Hurriyat did not help me but I hold no grudge against its leaders.'

Her business-like our demeanour is back when she talks of how she has rebuilt her life after her release.The fighter in her refused to let her remain bogged down by her jail sentence. She wanted a bigger profile than that of a woman who had been sent to collect funds for terrorists. It was not easy. While she was in prison the Hurriyat which she had joined in 1993, split. She decided to join the Geelani faction of the Hurriyat. In 2013, she founded the 'Kashmir-e-Tehreeke Khawateen' to work for Kashmiri prisoners in consultation with Geelani. 'I go to attend conferences in Geneva and highlight issues of Kashmiri prisoners.' She shows me videos on her computer of recent agitations by women in Awantipura and Burdhan (Srinagar)

14. *Prisoner No. 100*, p. 42.

demanding azadi for Kashmir which she organizes as an active member of the All Parties Hurriyat Conference (Geelani Group). As the shots of women shouting slogans appear on her computer screen, Zamarud's face lights up. 'I have always liked working for the cause of women and organizing women into action,' she explains when I comment on her apparent delight at seeing women protesters. 'It gives me a sense of purpose.'

The first dowry death in Anantnag in the late 1980s proved to be the trigger for Anjum Zamarud to turn activist to fight for women. At that time Zamarud was a teacher there in Hanifia College. A sportsperson with an outgoing personality, she was a popular figure. It was not difficult for the tall, slim and attractive Zamarud to gather support when she launched a women's welfare association. In a week she had collected 200 members. The agenda of the association was to launch an anti-dowry campaign, work for employment opportunities for women, put an end to paying bribes to get jobs, and their empowerment. Zamarud nostalgically recalls that both Hindus and Muslims came together under the banner of the association. They were school-goers, college students, teachers and even housewives.

Soon things changed. 'In 1989 militancy erupted and a teacher was killed in police firing. Our Hindu Pandit friends started to leave the Valley. The mohaul (atmosphere) changed. The call for azadi subsumed all other causes including concerns of women.' The texture of twenty-year-old Zamarud's activism too underwent a change. Her family home in Anantnag became a shelter for the boys in her extended family who had turned militants. 'Other boys too came looking for food, a place to sleep and hide arms.' Amongst them was JKLF commander Manzoor-ul-Islam. 'He was a distant relative and also my neighbour. My junoon for azadi had already started.' In the February of 1990 Anantnag saw 'the first and biggest crackdown by the security forces in Anantnag. I was picked up and taken by security forces to a hospital compound. I saw hundreds of boys lined up there, their face covered with their phirans. I was the only woman there. I was interrogated about Manzoor and instructed to inform when he visited next.' Anjum Zamarud refused point-blank.

By now Zamarud had been identified and accepted as part of the resistance movement. 'I was advised by Manzoor to involve women with the tehreek-e-azadi (movement for freedom).' Zamarud's face lights up as she recalls the enthusiasm of young girls of the area to join the struggle. 'At least 100 girls would come to me every day and say they wanted to join tehreek-e-azadi. The militants were heroes in our eyes. They used to show us AK-47s. This was the first time we saw AK-47s in Kashmir. The girls were charged up and wanted arms training to be able to take part in the armed struggle. They did not want their role to be restricted to arranging and providing militants with hideouts and food and going to visit the families of those martyred. During those days women who aided the boys were proud to do so and they earned the praise of their families and society for being so brave.'

Zamarud's house was constantly raided by security forces. 'I decided to go underground.' Zamarud went to Srinagar. By then she had forms signed by 1500 girls who were willing 'to do anything for the azadi struggle.' The forms detailed the blood group of the woman, the training in first aid and nursing they had received in hospitals under the control of militants and their level of competence in providing religious education. Manzoor advised her to involve these women with the movement. Zamarud along with three other women founded the Muslim Khwateen Markaz and was made its general secretary. 'I personally think that girls should not take up arms and instead work in their own dairaa (sphere) like leading protests, visiting the homes of martyred boys and carrying memorandums to the UN Kashmir Observer Group.' The Markaz members brought out a publication bearing the message of militancy and about the cause. Their work was also to prepare press releases and look after communications. Zamarud wrote extensively about young girls killed by, what was officially stated, 'unknown gunmen'.

Her experience during that time 'made me realize it is a man's world. I saw the arrogance of the militant leaders. They treated women like their subordinates. We didn't know then but the ranks had renegades and infiltrators who wanted to give the tehreek a bad name. These were uneducated, unemployed anti-social elements who took advantage of the movement to make space for themselves. These men exploited the women in the tehreek. This is one reason for the women taking a step back and becoming apprehensive about joining the movement.'

Zamarud herself 'moved away and changed the direction of the Markaz'. The agenda for her was set by the sight of the wailing mother of a fourteen-year-old boy who had 'disappeared'. The woman came to Zamarud seeking help to locate her son. 'She wanted me to use my contacts with the militants to find out if he had joined them or crossed over (to Pakistan). I was able to confirm that he had not gone across or joined the militants. We later had unconfirmed reports that he had been picked up by security forces.' The Markaz started to work for missing boys as by then 'boys had started to disappear.'

In 1993 the Hurriyat Conference gave a call for all separatist parties to come together on a common platform. She took the Markaz to the Hurriyat and 'I became a founding member of the Geelani faction of Hurriyat Conference though I was never given a place in the decision-making body.' Zamarud remained chairperson of the Markaz. She was also in the human rights cell of the Hurriyat and documented the 2001 rape victims in Kashmir. 'My focus has always been on women and working for related issues.'

On her return from jail, Zamarud could not go back to her work. The feisty Anjum Zamarud was struggling to overcome the trauma of days spent in prison. 'Though I was free and back home, I used to dread 6.00 p.m. It used to transport me back to the jail when every day we were locked in at that hour. I used to start shivering and felt I couldn't breathe. I did not have the confidence to even cross the street alone. I had nightmares.' Even the day she returned to her home in Srinagar she could feel little emotion. 'I did not even feel happy. I saw people coming to congratulate me. My sister was singing "Zamarud jannat ki noor hai". My family had stitched a new phiran for me but I just felt so detached from all that was happening around me. I was sad thinking of what I had made my family and specially my old mother go through.'

Did she regret she ever went to the Pakistan High Commission on that fateful day? Once again her voice is tinged with resentment. She gives no direct answer. Instead she tells me, 'I went to meet Jalil Abbas Jilani with a prior appointment because my party leader Abdul Ghani Butt (then chairman of the APHC [All Party Hurriyat Conference]) asked me to deliver some books to him. My main purpose was to get a visa to go to Pakistan to meet women's rights activists there before attending a workshop in Bangkok at the invitation of Alert International, a UK-based organization, in my capacity as head of the Muslim Khawateen Markaz, the womens' organization of the Hurriyat.' She makes no allegations but clearly, her resentment and bitterness emanates from a perceived sense of being framed. Does she resent she was tasked to deliver books to Jilani or that the Hurriyat did not plead with the Indian government for her release from prison as it had for others? 'It is a man's world. Let us leave it at that,' she says, and turns to autograph for me the book she has written about her days in prison.

Anjum Zamarud started to write *Prisoner No. 100* in 2008. It was a catharsis of sorts for her. 'Writing helped but my pen did not move as fast as my emotions and many things which I wanted to write got left out.' She decided to move on and joined Geelani's group of Hurriyat, the known hardline faction of the amalgamated Hurriyat Conference. On 25 November 2015, as reported by the Tribune New Service, Zamarud was appointed President of the Human Rights Committee of the Hurriyat Conference (G). I telephoned to congratulate her. Zamarud showed little excitement. 'I now have this immense responsibility on my shoulders. I am going to struggle hard to put an end to human rights violations in Kashmir.'

Zamarud has, like other women, been part of the azadi movement in the Kashmir Valley. In her opinion, women in Kashmir have played and continue to play a significant role by offering emotional and logistical support to the militants. According to her, the women of Kashmir encourage their men to go for jihad. A mother sheds no tears when her son makes the ultimate sacrifice. 'Women feel emotionally involved because they see the commitment of their menfolk and the sacrifices they make. They suffer when their innocent sons, husbands and brothers are picked up by security forces and disappear. They are angry at the injustice of it...the atrocities heaped on them. They want to fight for their men. At one stage they were prepared to take up arms and fight shoulder to shoulder with them but withdrew because they saw exploitation by bad elements which had infiltrated the tehreek.'

The now changed discourse of the movement is again seeing

a greater participation by young girls. 'Qualified engineers and well-educated boys are joining the separatist movement. They are a disciplined lot. This has again encouraged college-going girls to actively support the azadi tehreek though they are not taking up arms,' assesses Zamarud. Do the Kashmiri women have the temperament to take up the gun for combat? I ask. It takes a minute for Zamarud to answer. She nods her head to say 'no' then adds, 'Women here can't take up arms but do provide crucial support. A mother, sister and daughter stand with the militants emotionally. They can do anything for their men. Some get killed, some are tortured by security forces and some just disappear. There are such women in every village in Kashmir...not high-profile activists, but ordinary women who are extremely useful to militants as they provide them support for their operations.'

Khalida Akhtar

Anjum Zamarud could well have been talking of Khalida Akhtar.

In Paliharan village, Baramulla district, Khalida was just another schoolgirl till 21 January 2007. When the day began, no one knew that she was soon going to become the talk of the day and in fact many more to follow. It was nearing 8.00 a.m. and for 22-year-old Khalida, the start of just another regular day. Was it?

As always Khalida dressed with care for school that cold winter morning. She scrubbed her face clean. In keeping with Islamic dictates, she covered her white uniform with an ankle-long 'abaya'. Next she took the scarf, secured it tightly ostensibly to hide her lustrous dark brown hair. But she let a few errant locks tantalizingly peep out. One to always push the boundary a little further, she took some more liberties. With bold strokes she lined her almond-shaped eyes with charcoal black kajal. Then she brushed her lips ever so lightly with pink gloss. Was she living up to being called 'Preity Zinta', the Bollywood beauty of Kashmir? Her bhabi, Sweety, and schoolmates admiringly called her so. Even the boys in town called after her by that name.

Her mobile phone started to jangle as she stepped out to start her 4-5 km trek to the highway to catch a bus for the Government Girls Higher Secondary School in Baramulla. She quickened her pace so her family could not hear her phone conversation. Then she ran back to tell her bhabi not to worry if she was late returning home. After school she planned to consult a doctor for a boil erupting on her leg.

Then she was gone. Some eight hours later Khalida was found dead. She had a bullet-hole bang in the centre of her forehead. The police, working on information given by a passerby, came across her body in an apple orchard in Yar Bugh, Rafiabad, miles away and in the opposite direction of her Baramulla school. She was lying pale and motionless, the blood from the bullet wound already caked dry.

Khalida had not made it to school that day. She was standing at the Baramulla main bus stop near her school that morning when a Tata Sumo pulled up and whisked her away. A few standing around saw it happen but no one thought that noting down the registration number of the car was warranted. No one even reported the matter to the nearby Sheeri police station.

As dusk fell her mother, Saja, kept worry at bay by assuming that Khalida had decided to stay back at her elder sister Mumtaza's house in Dewan Bagh at Baramulla. She often did this. Her youngest brother, Sahil, had started to fret for his favourite sister. Then Saja noticed that Khalida had left behind the piece of embroidery she was working on. She always took it along when she was going to stay at her sister's place as she liked to work at it in her spare time.

A nagging fear started to envelop Saja. It was only a month ago that a warning note signed by 'the Hizbul Mujahideen boys' had been pinned to their gate. 'Khalida is a police informer,' said the letter. It ordered her to mend her ways or face the consequences. Her old father, Habibullah Dar, had found the note as he was leaving for the mosque for namaz. Her brothers had torn the paper and trashed it. But Saja and Habibullah Dar had not been able to forget it.

This was not the only reason for worry for Khalida's aged parents. Their Khalida had had many run-ins with the local police and had only a few day ago been released from prison. The police had accused her of links with her mama, her mother's brother, Ghulam Mohammad Lone, a militant with the LeT who had crossed over to Pakistan. After he was killed in 2001 in an encounter with security forces when he sneaked back into a village near Baramulla in Kashmir, police alleged that Khalida had maintained her links with militants introduced to her by Lone. Her handler now was a LeT commander, Abu Anar. Police records allege that Khalida was a LeT 'over-ground worker'. Her job was to carry messages and arms for its men. She also carried information relevant for their movement. She was booked by the police three times. Her three stints in prison caused a break in her education. Though in her twenties, she was still studying in Class 10.

Her first arrest was by the Baramulla police on 16 May 2002. She was charged with supporting crime. She was apprehended in old Baramulla town where she was with her mother and her brother Mohd. Yusuf Dar. After three hours they were allowed to go. Khalida was arrested and sent to Baramulla jail. She was released in 2003.

Her second arrest was a few months later in 2004, again by the Baramulla police. She was booked for eighteen months. After her release she went to live in the Nishat area of Srinagar. She returned to Baramulla in 2006. The Baramulla police and Handwara police arrested her for the third time later in the same year when she was allegedly on her way to Handwara to meet Abu Anar. He reportedly had a passport made for her to enable her to cross over to Pakistan. Khalida was arrested and sent to the Jammu district jail from where she was shifted to Srinagar jail by court orders and released in early January 2007.

Yet her family was not taken aback when at about 7.00 p.m., constable Ghulam Mohinuddin Khan knocked on their door. Khan was a neighbour. But what he said threw them into a state of shock. He said he had been telephoned by SHO Haider of Sheeri police post and tasked to inform them that their extrovert daughter, the beautiful young Khalida, had been shot dead.

The entire village went to see dead Khalida. She was lying in a police jeep, a blood-spattered shawl covering her pale face. A procession of stunned mourners brought her home and to her final resting place: 100 yards from her house, a simple unpretentious grass-covered mound of a grave in a corner of her elder brother's kitchen patch. It was enclosed with tin sheets to keep away stray dogs. For Khalida to rest in peace, barbed wires were put up to separate the grave from the dirt track. From her brother's hut which is barely a few steps away or even from the village road, Khalida's grave is an easy miss. It seems to have been kept as inconspicuous as possible as if by design. No one wants to talk about why Khalida may have been killed.

The day Khalida was killed the police allege she was on her way to meet the militant comrades of her uncle Ghulam Mohammad Lone at Rafiabad.

*

Eight years after Khalida was found dead, I arrive at her modest home. I know I will never be able to see her, meet her or get to know her as a person. She will not be able to tell me why she exchanged the life of an innocent schoolgirl for the perilous one of a terrorist's collaborator. I will never know if she was really working for her uncle's jihadi comrades or had turned police informer or worse, a double agent? Was she aware that the dangerous game she was playing could snuff out her young life? Yet, I want to see for myself the environment in which she lived and operated, hoping it will give me a peek into the world of women who are as lethal as any armed terrorist or militant in Kashmir without taking up the gun.

It is a sunlit day in total contrast to the fateful day Khalida began her last trip to school. There is no winter grey or any trace of snow on the trees. Instead red apples glowing like electric bulbs weigh down the trees in the orchards leading to her house. The fields add a dash of gold with their stacks of harvested rice and corn. The October cheer evaporates the moment Khalida's name is mentioned in the Habibullah Dar family home.

Her mother Saja starts to wail. She repeats what she has been saying for the last eight years in connection with Khalida's killing. 'Usko jhoota ilzam lagaya. Uska mama toh pehle hi Hamran Markoot (Rafiabad) mein security forces ke encounter mein maara gaya thaa...woh LeT ke saath thaa. Pakistan mein rahta thaa. Pehle hamare saath rehta thaa. Woh 2000 ke aas paas Pakistan ke group ke saath jihad ke liye chala gaya. Tab se hamne usko na dekha na baat ki. Woh yahan kabhi nahin aya. Khalida to bahut bacchi thi jab woh gaya. Woh uske saath kaise kaam kar sakti thi? Woh khoobsoorat thi na, iss liye ladke uska peecha karte the par woh unke taraf dekhti bhi nahin thi. Iss liye jhoota ilzam lagaya.' (They slapped false allegations against her. Her uncle had already been killed in an encounter with security forces in Hamran Markoot [Rafiabad]. He was with the LeT. He was living in Pakistan. He lived with us earlier. Around 2000 he went for jihad with a group from Pakistan. From then we had not seen or spoken to him. Khalida was a small child when he left...how could she have been working with him? She was beautiful, that is why boys used to follow her but she never even looked their way. That is why they made false allegations against her).

Who killed Khalida? Why was she shot? Who were these boys who followed her around? Are the police lying when they say she was on her way to meet Lone? The questions are met with incoherent babble from Saja. Then Khalida's bhabi Sweety takes over. Speaking for the family, she says they do not know who killed Khalida. Saja nods in assent when Sweety says that it was Khalida herself who had told them that she was often followed by boys in the town of Baramulla when she went to school. The family put this down to her good looks.

According to Sweety, the police too had told them that Khalida was in danger. After her release from the Jammu jail just a couple of weeks before she was shot dead, the police had suggested that Khalida should not return to her Paliharan home. 'Unho ne kaha ke usko hum naukri deynge. Usko Baramulla mein rehne do,' (they said they would give her a job, let her stay in Baramulla), says Sweety.

Out of concern for her safety, Khalida's parents urged her to stop going to school and stay home. But Khalida refused. 'Woh padhna chahti thi. Kehti thi ke naukri karoongi. Woh acchhi student thi' (she wanted to study. She said she wanted to work. She was good at studies), adds Sweety. Khalida also turned down her father's suggestion that she report to the police about the boys who followed her. 'Khalida kehti thi ke report karne se hum badnaam ho jayenge' (Khalida would say that if we report it will bring disrepute to us), Sweety tells me.

Saja glows with pride when she talks of Khalida's head-turning good looks. Sweety too talks of her sister-in-law being a 'modern bold' girl. She was the only one with a mobile phone and the most educated of them all. But Khalida had not shared her cell number with anyone in the family though they repeatedly asked for it. It is obvious that Khalida's number was known to others. 'Uske paas bahut phone aate the. Uske marne ke baad humne bahut poocha number ke bare mein. Phone bhi nahin mila' (she used to get many calls. After she died we asked many for her number. We could not even find the phone), informs Sweety.

The Habibullah family sees Khalida as a young, innocent beautiful girl maligned and targeted by ...they are not sure by whom. The men who pursued her or the police? All they say is 'Sab jhoota ilzaam lagaya uss par. Kaha mama ke saath connect hai. Woh ladko ke taraf mukateb nahi hoti thi to ilzaam lagaya. Woh Handwara pir baba ke paas gayi thi...har saal jatey hain... phir bhi pakada' (they made false charges against her. They said she had a connect with her uncle. They accused her because she paid no attention to the boys), rambles Saja. Sweety explains Saja's disconnected sentences are a result of how deeply she has been affected by Khalida's death. 'Humne uske sab photo hata diye. Agar Saja dekh leti hai to khana nahin khati hai.' (We have removed all her photographs. If Saja sees them she does not eat).

Since Khalida's death, Saja has been looking for information from representatives of some groups from Srinagar who come to offer condolence. 'Pata nahin kaun hain. Ek Mussalman ladki ayi thi. Aur log bhi aye...bus pooch-tach kar ke chale gaye. Koi madat nahi mili. Hamari zameen bhi salaab mein chali gayi' (we don't know who they are. A Muslim girl had come. Others came too... but left after making enquiries. Our land also was washed away in the flood), Saja laments. Habibullah is almost stone-deaf now. The moment Khalida's name is mentioned he takes out a worn-out much-thumbed file containing her death certificate and the FIRs filed against her. Can this give a clue as to why she was killed? he asks. The family wants to know why Khalida did not reach her school on 21 January 2007 and was found shot dead instead in an apple orchard in Dudan. I too would like to know. All I am left with is suspicion and speculation. Did the militants gun her down because they suspected she was double-crossing them? Or was she eliminated because the police feared she would pass vital information about them to which she was privy, to terrorists? Militants as well as the police in Kashmir allegedly eliminate those they become suspicious of. Khalida was not the first to be handed out this fate, nor will she be the last.

ARRESTS

1st arrest
16 May 2002, FIR No 91/2002. Charged under the Jammu and Kashmir State Ranbir Penal Code (RPC) Act 212. The Act applies to 'whoever harbours or conceals a person whom he knows or has reason to believe to be an offender, with the intention of screening him from legal punishment'. Released in November 2003

2nd arrest
2004, FIR No 138/2004. Charged under RPC Act 212. Released in August 2006

3rd arrest
September 2006, charged under RPC Act 212. Released early January 2007 from Jammu jail.

Died 21 January 2007

The Kashmiri women's participation in militancy in their 'watan' is not only limited to certain roles, but is a completely hush-hush affair. They themselves do not admit it to anyone, nor do the families. The high-profile names present themselves to the public as social activists, human rights crusaders and political activists while their work in some cases is directly or indirectly linked to facilitating terrorists and terror operations. Those who have the cover of anonymity do not need such screens. They just call themselves devout Muslims owing allegiance to jihad, or mujahideens and relatives fighting for the cause. The dictates of Islamic society do not give women the same status as men and this is reflected in Kashmir's Islamic militant as well as separatist outfits. The women accept subjugation as adherence to the social and religious norms they are governed by. Leaders of terrorist organizations recognize women as vital to keep their business going but do not allow them into their ranks. No Islamic militant outfit is known to date to have a women cadre. Women are sent out on dangerous assignments that often risk their lives without any qualms on the part of the men in terrorist outfits, but the gun, a frontline role and an exalted position in the organization's hierarchy is not for them to have. It is not permitted by Islam, argue militant as well as separatist leaders. Asiya Andrabi, the founding leader of the separatist Islamic group Dakhtaran-e-Millat (Daughters of the Nation) herself is of the opinion that a woman should not be tasked with anything that will expose her body as it is unIslamic. That is why a Muslim woman should be kept out of combat or never used as a human bomb because post-operation, her dead body will be exposed to all.

CHHATTISGARH

Bangles and Bayonets

'A hand wielding a gun has no place for bangles. If there is place it is only for self-confidence.'

—*Tulsi Murami*, Commander,
Local Guerilla Squad, Military Wing

THE WOMEN INVOLVED IN SUBVERSIVE ACTIVITY IN Kashmir and those in Chhattisgarh, a state in the centre-east of India in the grip of Left Wing extremism for over two decades, are a study in contrast. Not only do they look very different (the former, slim, fair with chiselled features and the latter, dusky and buxom), but even their psyche is at total variance. While the dissimilarity in their physical appearance can be attributed to several factors, the difference in their mindset is the result of two factors—one cultural and the other political. The Kashmiri women are restricted by conservative societal and rigid religious norms. The women militants in Chhattisgarh are from a tribal social milieu, which permits them choices and freedom. Unlike the women in Kashmir, they are part of terrorist organizations run in accordance with Maoist ideology, in which gender and class equality is inbuilt. Equality with men comes naturally to them from both quarters. For the women in Maoist groups operating in Chhattisgarh, being a militant is no cloak-and-dagger business or back alley activity. They live like the men and with them in jungle camps, take pride in handling sophisticated arms, are unflinching killers, participate in ambush and combat, make effective educators of Maoist ideology and are committed operators by choice. Tasks in the camp and assignments are shared equally by men and women. Exploitation of women, sexual or otherwise, is an exception in Maoist camps. In fact, women feel secure in their camps and hideouts. They feel empowered receiving a gun and a uniform. Women from the tribal belts of Chhattisgarh join the Maoist ranks and return home without fear of social ostracization or stigma. The only reason their families and they themselves keep it quiet is because of fear of security agencies. For most young girls, going off with Maoists is usually not a well-contemplated step. It is more than often taken nonchalantly, to try out something different from a dreary community existence. They look upon being a militant as an enjoyable experience to be given up in time for marriage and bearing children. Bhima is no different.

Bhima, *Motivator, Naxal Education Wing*

Bhima sings a strange lullaby. Instead of a soothing melody, the words are set to a vigorous marching tune better suited to spurring the child into action, than lulling her to sleep. She pats her daughter to the beat of the spirited refrain. 'Yeh gaon hamara, yeh gali hamari, yeh basti hamari, hal chale ke hamne fasal ugaya, kheton ko jagaya, din raat jaga kar fasal ugaya, apne bina dhaan nahin, dahi nahi, doodh nahi, chalo re, garib, mazdoor, kisan miljul ke rahena re, krantikaari jhande tale, sanghatan mein rahena re, yeh looteron ko laat maro, hata do re.' (This village is ours, this street is ours, this settlement is ours, we have used the plough to grow crops, we have awakened the farms, by staying awake night and day we have cultivated, without us there is no paddy, no curd, no milk. Come on, the poor, labourer, farmer, live together under the banner of revolution. Stay in the organization. Kick out the looters, remove them).

The two-room brick tenement in a quiet part of Jagdalpur, headquarter of Bastar district in Chhattisgarh, reverberates with the song of the rebels. The little girl falls asleep. Her mother sings it to her every night. It is familiar so it is comforting. She doesn't understand the words. Nor has Bhima explained them to her.

The song was brought to the tribal swathes of Madhya Pradesh in central India by Naxalites, far Left radicals, (commonly called Maoists and Naxalwadis in Chhattisgarh), waging a protracted people's war against the Indian government in the late 1980s. As a fourteen-year-old, Bhima heard the song evening after evening from men who came to her village, Jagargunda in Sukma district, from the adjoining state of Andhra Pradesh. Jagargunda, like many other villages, was a forgotton one. There was no presence of security men. No roads, no electricity, no medical care. The village school had no teachers. The only authority was the forest guard and land revenue officer. The Naxals were kings. They controlled the forest, which the tribals had considered their own for generations.

By 1992, Naxal leaders based in Andhra Pradesh had started visiting border villages of Madhya Pradesh to spread their class struggle. Sukma district was amongst the first few they infiltrated as it shared a border with insurgency-infested Andhra. They were welcomed by the locals living in abject poverty, untouched by development or gifts of modernity. To add to their misery, they felt they were at risk of losing their right over accessing the forest for their daily needs as had been the tradition for centuries. Forest guards not only prevented them from foraging in the forests, but demanded a share from their gatherings to grant them permission to hunt for food, fuel and medicinal herbs. These outsiders from Andhra were offering them a solution. Their songs and lectures urged them to rebel, fight for their rights and overthrow the government. Unlike the government outsiders, these men were their friends. But communication was difficult as the visitors from Andhra spoke only Telugu, a language foreign to the tribes of Madhya Pradesh. The Naxals started to recruit locals to spread their word. The first lesson was learning the Telugu language. The village people readily accepted them as leaders and started to go to Naxal camps for training. Bhima, all of fourteen years, went too. 'Bahut log ja rahe the, main bhi chali gayi. Maa baap ko batai bina.' (Lots of people were going [with the Naxals], I also went with them without telling my mother and father).

Bhima had been with the Naxals for three years when she heard a song she knew well by now sung at a Konta village meeting. As usual she was moved by the words. But it was the singer who made a greater impression on Bhima. As a motivator or educator, she had attended many meetings of villagers to tell them about the Naxal fight against the government and urge them to join the organization. The song was sung at every meeting. But this singer had electrified the words with his baritone. She had to clutch her rifle, given to her when she joined the Naxal ranks, tight, as his voice was propelling her to go and hunt down the looterey (looters) carrying off the forest produce to the big city.

Bhima spoke to Ramesh in Telugu, a language they had been taught at the Naxal camp in Andhra. She thought he hailed, like all senior Naxal leaders then, from Andhra Pradesh. To her surprise, he told her he was from Jarpalli village, in Bijapur district, one of the first entry points for the Andhra Naxals. Like many youngsters in his area, fifteen-year-old Ramesh provided food and shelter to the men in uniform who came promising to help the poor. In 1989, three years before Bhima, moved by the Naxal rhetoric, had run away with them, Ramesh enrolled as a member of the Communist Party (Marxist-Leninist) People's War Group.

For Bhima, the name did not matter. All she knew was that she was going away with 'dada log' (big brother), the name the Naxals where known by in the tribal villages of Madhya Pradesh. She was not the only girl in the dalaan (group) she was sent to. Of the twenty members, there were fifteen girls. But Bhima was scared of living in a forest camp. It meant a nomadic existence, constantly on the move and making camp under trees for shelter. Water had to be fetched from a nearby stream or pond. One's bed was a thin polythene sheet. If it rained, tarpaulin was strung across branches to provide a shelter of sorts. Worse was the fear of snakes and scorpions. The military book, according to which they were trained to exercise and use arms, did not teach them how to deal with this danger. Bhima soon learnt that the best way out was to lie as still as a log if there was a rustle of a snake movement.

Bhima's job was to spread the word. This did not scare her. She moved from village meeting to village meeting fearlessly. 'Uss time mein koi police nahi thi. Gaonwalle hamare saath the. Khana paani milta tha aur hamare saath chal padte the.' (At that time there was no police presence in the remote villages. The people there were with us. They gave us food and water and were willing to come along with us). Once or twice Bhima and her comrades had to abandon meetings and run when they were informed that security patrols were on the main highway or in close proximity to the village. Since the Naxals wore olive green uniforms they could be easily detected from amongst the village folk.

As Ramesh sang at the 1995 Kota meeting, he was just wrapping up his schedule for the day. He saw a short, round-faced teenager in combat gear, looking at him in rapt attention. He was used to it. His cadre members always did so. He did not know her by name, but he was aware of her as a Naxal motivator. When she stepped forward to talk to him at the end of the programme, he realized there was more than just 'comradely' interest. Bhima and Ramesh made it a point to meet up daily at the camp.

Love blossomed amongst guns, grenades and jhaad (tree). After every ambush, Bhima was relieved to see Ramesh return alive and without injury. It was not always an ambush that had her on edge. Ramesh would often disappear from camp for days without informing her where he was going. She knew he was bound by the rules not to inform her. But she knew he was on a risky mission of either ambushing a police patrol to snatch their arms or negotiating a buy from them. These were the sources of arms for the Naxals. At times she sat with him as he assembled 12-bore guns, .303 rifles and country-made pistols.

Bhima was also given a pistol to tuck into her belt. She never did get the chance to use it. Her assignment was to hold meetings in villages to popularize the slogan 'punjipati ko bhagao, road banao, talab banao' (chase away the trader, build a road, dig a pond). But she hesitated to sing after she had heard Ramesh do so. 'Uske tarah koi nahin gaa sakta. Uske awaz mein shakti hai. Aaj bhi...' (No one can sing like him. There is power in his voice. Even today...).

Ramesh's voice carries through Bhima's window. He has joined her cradle song. Bhima stops singing. His powerful voice, now lowered to a soft pitch, is yet again drawing her like a magnet. She tucks the mosquito net under her sleeping daughter and walks up to the mantelpiece in the room. Carefully, she picks up a framed photograph from it, wipes it with the pallav of her sari and comes out. 'Hamari shaadi ki hai' (our wedding photograph), she says in a voice brimming with tenderness. I look at it. It is an unusual wedding picture. The bride and groom are both dressed in battle fatigues, each holding a .303 rifle. The vermilion smear on Bhima's forehead looks out of place with the rather severe attire.

Bhima and Ramesh married in 1995 in the Konta Naxal camp. The ceremony was presided over by Gopanna, the camp commandant. He directed them to exchange their guns. The wedding rituals were over. Then it was time for the vows. No children while in camp, party and organization work should not suffer because of wedlock. The last and most harsh was, no tears if either of them was killed during operations. Was Bhima comfortable with the vows and the ceremony? 'The day we decide to join the Naxals, we know we are entering a world which is different. We are no longer bound by the rules of the outside world.' Not having children was the easiest vow to keep, she says. Ramesh, like all other men in the camp, had undergone surgery for sterilization.

In accordance with Maoist camp practice, Ramesh was transferred to another makeshift hideout. Married couples are not allowed to stay together in the same group for long. Pining for loved ones is usual in an encampment. Love letters are often sent with other 'official' missives through a hand-to-hand secure postal system used by Maoists in the jungles. A cache of correspondence recovered by a police team from a Maoist hideaway following an operation in the Doditumnar area of Dantewada district in January 2018, included personal messages besides internal status reports, information on police deployment, difficulties in some divisions and the need to procure essentials like mobile phone batteries. These personal letters give a glimpse of the emotional side of the militants. An unnamed writer has written in Gondi language to a 'Kumari behen' asking how she is and hoping she is happy. Probably a forlorn lover, he goes on to ask, 'Why don't you ever write me a letter? We met once at that place, but even then you did not come to my dera to sit with me.' What follows in the letter indicates that talk of marriage has caused trouble in the blossoming relationship. Entreating Kumari behen not to consider matrimony, he writes, 'We knew about all this when we entered the party. We should not get angry when these small and big problems come. If you fall ill, take some pills and learn from the political military school.' He goes on to exhort her not to contemplate leaving the organizaton. 'We should not think about returning home... If there are problems, you should narrate this at the branch meeting and fix the issue.' Another letter found in the bag left behind by fleeing Maoists is from a man trying to trace a woman comrade who has apparently caught his fancy in a world where names are constantly changed for security reasons. He asks, 'There used to be a Paiki who was with you. Where is she now? Has she kept the same name or has she changed it?'[15]

News that trickled in from home made Bhima sad. Her husband was in another camp and she did not have him around for comfort. Within the span of a year she heard of the death of her mother, then her brother followed by her sister-in-law. Bhima wept every night. She could not forgive herself for being the reason for her parents being summoned often to the district police station. They were interrogated on her disappearance. After eight years in the Naxal camp, Bhima was homesick. She talked to Ramesh, and they decided on leaving the camp.

But Ramesh was denied permission by his commander, Gopanna. Bhima returned to her village home alone and surrendered to the police. To cover Ramesh's tracks, he was transferred by the leadership to a camp in Minagatta, some distance from Konta. The police were on his heels.

Bhima knew she was under police watch because of Ramesh. She had received information that her husband would visit her that night. Bhima left her hut and slipped away to another for a rendezvous with her husband. As expected, the police arrived

15. *The Indian Express*, 26 March 2018.

and raided her home. Ramesh had a narrow escape, leaving behind a very concerned wife. Ramesh was aware that the net would close in any day. He yearned to be with his wife. He had also learnt that Bhima had been arrested and was in jail for subversive activity. Ramesh spoke to his sister to negotiate with the police. If he gave himself up to the police, would they withdraw the cases against him? In the late 1990s, the state government was already considering offers to militants that would be incentive enough for them to come over-ground and lay down arms. To 'surrender' was an option but the details were still sketchy. In 2000, Ramesh surrendered to the Dantewada police, after several rounds of back and forth between his sister and the police. Ramesh wanted to make sure that he was not being trapped and once he surrendered he would be able to be with his wife. He wanted to fulfil his wife's wish to have a home and child. He was hailed as a big catch.

Ramesh and Bhima were able to meet only in June 2001 after he had served a jail term of more than a year and a half. They desperately wanted to have a home together, start a family and lead a 'normal' life. The first step was a visit to the Raipur hospital for reversing sterilization. But things did not settle down for eight years. The police gave them a plot and some money to construct a house, but they needed a steady source of income. 'Aath saal bahut museebat thi. Koi permanent naukri nahi thi. Ramesh mali ka kaam karta tha par permanent nahi tha.' (For eight years we had to bear a lot of trouble. There was no permanent job. Ramesh worked as a gardener but he was not made a permanent employee). But Bhima did not once think of returning to the Naxal group. Nor did they contact her. 'Woh sab khatam. Sab peeche chodh diya hum dono ne.' (All that was finished. We had left it behind us). Bhima now is finally content. She is an assistant constable in the police department and Ramesh has a permanent government job. Once again she has a uniform, but the job is very different to what she did as a Naxal. She has friends and colleagues who are aware of her past. 'Unko iss baat se matlab nahin na unko farak padta hai.' (They are not bothered about it nor does it concern them). More than her, they are in awe of Ramesh. 'Yeh bahut senior leader tha. Iske sar par award tha.' (He was a very senior leader. He carried an award on his head). Often people gather at his house to ask him to sing. There is always an encore and Ramesh obliges with the song of the rebels. The biggest source of happiness for them is their six-year-old daughter. We live for her, she is the star of our life, they tell me. She is their future.

The only remnant of the past is the carefully preserved wedding photograph showing them in uniform and with their guns. But the song they sing every evening also holds their past. To it is tied many a sweet memory. Bhima knows someday she will have a lot to explain to her daughter. She often points to the photograph and asks 'tumhare bandook kahan hai' (where are your guns)? Bhima has decided that when the question gets persistent 'tab mein usko gane ka matlab batlaungi.' (I will explain the words of the song to her then).

Tulsi Murami, *Commander, Local Guerilla Squad, Military Wing*

As Bhima sings to her daughter, 29-year-old Tulsi listens to the music of her bangles. Blood red, turquoise blue, fluorescent green and mustard yellow dusted with gold. The glass bangles go up from her wrists, almost reaching her elbows. They clink softly as she moves, the bold hues contrasting with her dusky hands. The tinkle mingles with her irrepressible giggles to create a jingle of its own. Tulsi is absorbed in the melody. She looks down at her wrists and runs her fingers over her bangles. The sound appears to mesmerize her. I wait till she has had enough of it. Slowly she looks up and chuckles again. It is actually an embarrassed laugh. Then Tulsi goes all coy, pulls her pink sari tightly across her narrow shoulders, stretches out her hands in a gesture of mock helplessness. 'Kya karoo, choodi bahut acchi lagti hain.' (What should I do? I love glass bangles).

Glass bangles and feeling helpless are luxuries Tulsi denied herself for fourteen long years. 'Jab haath mein bandook hai tu choodi ki jagha nahin. Jagha hai to bas apne mein bharose ki.' (A hand wielding a gun has no place for bangles. If there is place it is only for self-confidence). The tough talk does not match Tulsi's delicate looks. She oozes femininity. A long dark braid dances sensually on her waist accentuating its narrow span. Her kohl-lined eyes and a glittering bindi on her forehead complete the picture of a demure belle. What a dialogue, I exclaim in mock appreciation. She answers with her signature giggle. In a voice so soft that she has to be repeatedly told to speak up she accepts 'drama walla dialogue to hai par sachayi yehi hai' (it is dialogue suited for a drama but this is the truth).

Drama and colour have always fascinated her. Tulsi found plenty of it when, as a fourteen-year-old, she watched stage performances by groups of men and women who had been visiting her village in Bijapur district for the last couple of years. It was 2000 and the Andhra Pradesh police by now was hot on the heels of Naxalites based there. They were being chased out of their base camps in Andhra and had for almost a decade been regular visitors to villages inhabited by the Gond, Rajgond, Dhurwa, Madiya and Muriya tribes. The tribal belt of Madhya Pradesh since November 2000 had become a part of the newly founded state of Chhattisgarh. The thickly forested Bastar area of Chhattisgarh where 70 per cent of the population belonged to various tribes had already become a source of recruits for their fighting force. From amongst them they had developed a second line of command. The land here was fertile in more ways than one. Oppression and exploitation of tribesmen by moneylenders, patwaris (land department officials) and government guards was on the increase. They were losing their right to the forest on which they were traditionally dependent for food, fuel, medicine and daily drink. Rebellion was brewing in the tribal land of the new state of Chhattisgarh.

Tulsi was blissfully unaware of all this. All she knew was that she loved to watch the Naxals dance and sing. She was taken up by their songs of revolution, lively folk dances and khel (plays) that staged the story of their villages. The theme was always exploitation of the tribals, urging them to rebel against the government exploiters. Her village, Taklore, in Bijapur district, was one of the first few to be targeted by the Naxal leadership, being contiguous to Andhra Pradesh (now part of the newly founded state of Telengana).

Tulsi worked the black fertile soil at her farm without tiring. Sowing was not a hard task. All she had to do was scatter rice on it and it would take root to produce enough of a crop to feed her parents and her brother. But the monotony was getting to her. She looked forward to the evening show of song and dance by the 'dada log'. One particular evening in the winter of 2000 the programme was followed by an announcement. The sanstha (organization) was going to open a new dalaan (wing).

The girl sitting next to Tulsi in the audience felt her friend nudge her. 'Chalein?' Tulsi asked with a giggle. Without informing their parents, the teenagers decided to go with the Naxal band. They too would sing and dance and stage plays. So they thought.

People often took Tulsi's habit of giggling as a sign of her being a giddy-headed girl. The Naxal leader of the camp in Ikool village in Narayanpur district, Orchha tehsil, was not one to be misled. Her chuckles only masked her real self. He saw her as calm and self-assured. He noticed her confidence while dealing with the unexpected in the camp kitchen. When the tea boiled over, Tulsi giggled but quickly swung into action to restart the fire and fill the pot with fresh water. She never flapped when they found the rice tin empty or even when the water container leaked dry in the middle of the night. She just giggled and quickly looked for a way out. Tulsi stood out from amongst the fifteen other freshly recruited girls assigned to peel vegetables, scrub pots and pans and cook. Her friend could not take camp life in the forest. She fled with a man she wanted to marry. Tulsi burst into uncontrollable giggles when she learnt of it. We had left home to have fun and excitement, she told her camp mates with a laugh. Tulsi stayed on. A month later she was dispatched to the camp in Kohkameta village.

It changed her. For one, Tulsi had to learn to repress her giggle. If she did not, it could mean death. She was now the commander of the local guerrilla squad. A laugh during combat action was a sure giveaway. Even the slightest sound could attract an enemy bullet. Many a time she did want to burst into laughter but managed not to do so. Once while in hiding waiting to ambush a CRPF (Central Reserve Police Force) patrol she had to stuff her mouth with a scarf to stop a telltale laugh. The CRPF squad obviously had intelligence about the presence of the Naxals. They too were in hiding waiting to pounce on them. Tulsi had taken position behind a boulder. A few feet below her perch she spotted a policeman silently crawling on the ground to reach the spot from where he could take aim. He was unaware of the Naxals above him. 'Mushkil se hansee roki. Roomal muh mein bhara aur fire kiya. Woh ghayal hua.'

(With difficulty I stopped myself from laughing. I stuffed my mouth with a handkerchief and fired. He was injured). Tulsi laughs at the memory. 'Woh policewalla itna buddhu lag raha tha' (the police guy was looking so silly), she says by way of explanation.

Within a year of being recruited she became a sought-after member of the Naxal Military Wing. Posted to Platoon 1 stationed in Abhujmad in Narayanpur district and promoted as Member, Area Committee, her assignments ranged from mundane kitchen work, to sentry duty and taking part in ambushes. The Iragbatti (Narayanpur district) encounter in 2000 was her real-time classroom. Tulsi shed her fear of firing in half an hour without using the gun. During the ambush, Tulsi sat at a distance and calmly watched the police and her comrades exchange fire. She had been sent only to watch and learn. She saw them gun down one policeman. The takeaway for Tulsi had little to do with handling of firearms. It did not matter which gun she had. She had to remember to always shoot with confidence. There is no time to hesitate and doubt one's ability. If you don't get them, they will get you.

The .303 rifle exploded. It was Tulsi's first shot ever. The Lairi village (Chhattisgarh–Maharashtra border) operation came a few days after her lessons at Iragbatti, but firing came easily to her. Her team comprising three platoons of Naxals, around 70-80 men and women in all, had been taken by surprise by the police exploding bombs on the road. But she did not allow it to ruffle her. She stood her ground and fired with confidence. Did her first shot find its mark? I ask. She is not sure. All she can recall is that the firing left three policemen dead.

Three years after leaving home Tulsi returned to her village, Taklore. It was no celebratory homecoming. Her parents, in search of her from the day she did not return after an evening show of song and dance, were not even aware that she had come to the village school. It was the dead of a summer night. The CRPF had made its first-ever camp in Bastar in the school. Tulsi and thirty of her people had come for them. They opened fire on the men sleeping outside, killing three. As the men scrambled for cover, Tulsi melted into the darkness. She led her comrades through familiar paths out of the scene of shooting. These were the lanes she had so often walked with her friends to the patch of land she cultivated. She knew the shortcut to the forest where she went to collect herbs and firewood. In fact Tulsi had been deliberately chosen for the Taklore assignment because it was her own village where she had played and wandered around and knew every inch. You carried out a massacre in your home village? I ask incredulously. Did you not feel odd?

'Nahi....jab sanghatan mein the toh mera gaon jaisa kuch dimag mein nahi aata. Bus kaam karna hai yehi dimag mein rehta hai'. (No. When in the organization, things like my village don't cross your mind. All you have in mind is that you have a task to finish).

*

The thin polythene sheet under her was again damp with her sweat. The breeze seemed to bypass her tormented body. Her head was throbbing with pain. Tulsi could not even groan. Nor could she toss and turn too often. The smallest of sounds carried far in the night of the forest. It could jeopardize the camp and give away its location. This was not the first time that Tulsi had the severe headache which affected only one side of her head. Earlier it came once in a couple of months. Now it had become a daily nuisance.

Tulsi left the Naxals with whom she had spent fourteen eventful years. She told them she was too sick to be of any use to them. She wanted rest. She wanted to be nursed by her father and mother. Tulsi trudged through the forest to the main highway. On the outskirts of a village, an accompanying comrade arranged for a sari for her. Don't forget to get some bangles, all normal girls wear bangles, she told the person who was to procure her a change of clothes so that she could discard her uniform. A Naxal contact in the village returned soon with her shopping list.

Few in the local bus gave the sari-clad girl a second glance. Like other women she wore many bangles and a simple sari. Tulsi was not scared of being detected. How was anyone to know she was a Naxal guerrilla on sick leave? As the bus rumbled along the potholed road, Tulsi could only think of a reunion with her father and mother. But time had taken a toll.

Her father had died. Her mother too was not there. The hut which had been her home till she was fourteen years old stood empty. The village folk looked at her as she sat alone in the hut. It was news of her father's death that she found hard to accept. Had he died heartbroken because of her? Their consolations only made her feel worse. The tears soon found a voice. They turned into sobs when she heard that the dada log came often and harassed her parents. Why, wondered Tulsi. Why should they do this when she was putting her life on the line for the sanghatan. She had become one of them, hadn't she?

When darkness spread its cloak around her, Tulsi saw the flicker of an oil lamp. A concerned neighbour brought light. He told her that her mother had shifted to Bacheli village. Things had moved on while Tulsi had been living in the forest with the Naxals, eager to see which new gun she would be given next to handle. She had used the heavyweight 12-bore which she had to reload after every two shots while bullets flew around her, graduated to a .303 rifle and then the more efficient self-loading rifle. Much to her regret she was not given the chance to use the lethal AK-47. It was usually handled by men.

It was news of her kid brother that jolted Tulsi out of her reverie. He had become a man and joined the state police force. Something happened to her stomach. It was a sensation alien to Tulsi during all her years as an outlaw. Fear sucked at her innards like an iron grip pulling her heart, lungs and intestines to the bottom of her stomach. Her little brother, who had run to her when in trouble and proudly showed her the birds he carved out of wood, had now become a danger to her life. He meant arrest and jail for Tulsi. The middle-aged man looked at the fast diminishing oil in the lamp. He had no more to tell her. Nor did he have any questions. Like the others, he knew Tulsi had gone away with the Naxals as had many other young boys and girls after her. The Naxals suspected that her brother would pass on information about his sister's whereabouts and lead security agencies to their hideouts, the neighbour told her. The families of those who had disappeared into the forests usually received fragments of news of them. Sometimes messages were sent through sympathizers in the area. At times sightings were reported by village folk on their way to the haat (local weekly bazaar) or out in the jungle to tap the tall palm trees for the liquid it oozes to make selfee, a local drink that turns alcoholic when fermented in a clay pot.

Her mother stood at the door of the hut and watched Tulsi hurrying towards her. She did not run out to welcome her daughter whom she had not seen for more than a decade. It did not surprise Tulsi. Her mother had a right to be angry with her for running away from home. But she was taken aback when the anger in her mother's voice was replaced by panic. Go away, she was shouting. Go away or the police will come after you. Your life will be spent in jail, her mother screamed. But

Tulsi continued to move towards her. She collapsed in a heap at her mother's feet, too tired and sick to walk a step further. She was finished with being on the run.

*

The young man had a tough decision to make when he saw his sister after many years. As a policeman it was his duty to report her to the law enforcement agency. Yet could he actually do it? Yes, she was a member of the banned outfit but she was his sister too. He took Tulsi aside and had a long chat with her. Sitting under a tree, chatting away as twilight crept upon them, it seemed a replay of times gone by. Please surrender to the government. Lay down arms otherwise they will come for you. It is a matter of time before they catch you and dump you in jail. What will be your life then, he asked, hoping Tulsi would see sense. If you surrender, you have a future ahead, advised her brother. You will also be able to consult a doctor for your headache.

The future did turn out to be good. Tulsi surrendered in September 2014 in Jagdalpur. Her bouts of headache vanished. She was given a government job. Tulsi does not want to give details of where she works and what her job entails. She wants to talk about her colleague whom she met at her new workplace and married in 2015. He lives in another town. They are waiting to be transferred to the same place so they can start a family. Till then they have to be content meeting once a month. Guess what he brings for her on every visit. Glass bangles!

Kamla Pulsum, *Deputy Commander, All Woman Ambush Team, CPI (Maoist), Chhattisgarh*

Like Bhima and Tulsi, Kamla too loves the songs of rebellion. 'Mawa nate, mawa raj' (My land, my right), sang fourteen-year-old Kamla along with her classmates. The hair on her arms stood up. Colour started to creep up her dimpled cheeks. Her voice reached a ferocious tenor. Suddenly there was a catch in her throat, emotions almost strangulating her voice. Yes, these were the exact words Kamla would have liked to spit out to challenge the overbearing government agents breathing down the neck of her people. Could the lyrical exhortations taught by visiting teams of Naxals be the mantra to take on forest guards and moneylenders who harassed them when they went to collect food and firewood from the deep lush forest in which stood the cluster of huts called Grambasin?

It was just another day in the Grambasin village school. There were no studies. In 2002, Grambasin like other tribal settlements in Narayanpur district of central India's Chhattisgarh state, was under virtual control of the Naxalites. The village grapevine across the tribal belt of Chhattisgarh jangled not only with news of deadly Naxal attacks on security forces but also with grim stories of how they killed detractors and government informers. The Grambasin school circumspectly adhered to the Naxal diktat. Study hours meant singing of rebellion, of a fight against oppression and for the rights of the Adivasis.

It was a tall, fair by Gond tribal standards, sprightly teenager who ran to welcome the Naxal motivators when they came to the Grambasin school on their regular weekly visit to talk to the teachers and children. Kamla was eagerly waiting for them. For some months now she had stopped enjoying the folk litany she sang with her mother when they beat the chaff off the rice grain. Even when she sang, she was troubled by questions.

Why sing praise of the bounty of the forest which was now being denied to them by 'outsiders', Kamla asked herself. The government was siphoning away the produce and she could no longer gather honey and medicinal herbs without fear of the forest guard. Her father had to now go like a thief to collect mahua flowers from the trees in the forest, to make the local intoxicating brew. And why sing of goddess Dhanteshwari, the deity worshipped by the Gonds? What good had she done for her people?

Kamla was awake the night she overheard her mother talk to her father about finding a husband for her. No, that was her right. Gond girls traditionally picked their men. That was the custom. Why was this right being snatched away from her? she asked her mother next morning. All she got as an answer was a long hard stare. Kamla stared back with defiance. She heard her mother mutter about the ghotul, the traditional tribal village dormitory where unmarried men and women were sent to live together, to get a taste of married life before they took the plunge with partners of their choice, no longer being the best option. A marriage arranged by her father would be best. But Kamla was determined. She was going to make her own choices in her life.

The woman who spoke to them that morning in school was not a Gond nor was she from Chhattisgarh. She had come through the forest from adjoining Gadchiroli, a district in Maharashtra state. For almost a decade now, Naxals had started to push themselves into Gadchiroli from the state of Andhra Pradesh (now Telengana) with which it shared a border at its other end. The Gadchiroli route was one of the routes they had been taking to infiltrate the Adivasi villages in Chhattisgarh. The impoverished and exploited tribal villagers began to look at them for redemption. The Naxals started to recruit them for their fighting force while keeping the leadership in Andhra Pradesh hideouts. To reach out to the tribals they learnt their language and their lifestyle.

Kamla knew the Naxal didi would speak to them in their Gondi dialect. She had made them aware of many new things, like their rights on the forest they lived in and the right to action against government agents. There was another new Kamla noticed today. Looking at the didi she suddenly became conscious of her own bare shoulders and arms. Like all Gond women, Kamla had deftly covered her breasts with one end of her sari, securing it round her waist. Didi wore a stitched blouse though the paata (sari) was the same off-white, the border coloured maroon with a dye the locals made from the bark of a tree. Before she could give it further thought, Didi seemed to be answering her unvoiced questions. The Naxal motivator was urging the teenagers to take things into their hands to rise out of abject poverty, to fight the state oppressors and for their right to their land and forest. No one could help them but themselves. Not even their Dhanteshwari. Kamla was convinced.

They came for her a year later. She was fifteen.

Six years later Kamla was a trained killer. 'I am an ace shot. I never miss my target,' she tells me with pride. The olive green fatigues, the uniform of the Naxalite cadre, became her daily wear.

It was a woman in trousers and shirt with a camouflage print that the policeman saw running down the road straight towards him in 2008. He was riding a motorcycle. Behind him was a posse of eleven men. The noon sun beat down on them as they rode down the Mardapal village strip of a road to the marketplace. For a fraction of a second he was taken aback when he saw the woman was pointing a .303 rifle at him. He reached for his gun. Kamla fired first. The bullet hit him on his head. She had shot him dead. What was your first thought when you killed him? I ask. 'Sochne ka time nahin tha.' (There was no time to think). Kamla's shot was the cue for the rest of the Naxal ambush team to swing into action. They took over the firing, killing nine policemen in one hour.

Kamla relives the incident. Recalling the excitement of the action turns her cheeks red. She straightens her back, stands up with her legs parted and takes up an imaginary SLR. She points it at me and looks me straight in the eye. The tone of pride still holds in her voice. 'I was assigned to open fire first.' The camp leader had put her in the first line of fire because he wanted to take advantage of the element of surprise Kamla would prove for the policemen. Women participating in Naxal militant action at that time were a novelty for security men.

While hiding in a ditch bordering the road, Kamla was all ears for the sound of an approaching motorcycle. It came after three days.

With a quick well-practised leap Kamla jumped out of the ditch and ran head-on towards the approaching motorcycle. I have only a second, she told herself. Otherwise I will die. Kamla sensed the moment more than she actually saw it. The policeman stared at her instead of going for his gun. Kamla fired. The assessment report made by seniors in the team for the leaders stated that Section Commander Kamla had carried out her assignment to perfection.

What if the policeman had been quick with his gun and shot her instead? Kamla shrugs her shoulders in a matter of fact way. 'Mar sakte the.' (Could have died). Then as if to explain why things turned out in her favour she adds, 'par hamne teen din rehearsal kiya tha' (but we had rehearsed for three days before the ambush). In fact, life in her camp set up in the forest that ringed villages, including Mardapal, had been filled with planning for the ambush a month before. The moment the leaders received intelligence that a party of policemen went daily from their camp to the Mardapal market, they started to plan an ambush. A team of 100 which included ten women was formed. 'Mujhko planning achi lagti hai. Har kaam ko ache tareeke se karna chahhiye.' (I like planning. Everything should be executed in a proper way). As a member of the team Kamla made a map of the area detailing which side the policemen would come from, worked out ways to stop their motorbikes and undertook several reconnaissances of the spot to decide where they would ambush them. On the given date the ambush party took positions behind bushes, boulders and in ditches from 5.00 a.m. before the villagers could spot them.

The police team did not come that day. As the ambush team waited for them fear gripped Kamla. How was she to answer the call of nature? 'Bathroom jane ki jagha nahi thi. Aadmi to kahi bhi khade ho jate the. Hum aurat kya karte. Mein darke mare din bhar paani nahi peeti thi.' (There was no place to relieve myself. The men would just stand anywhere. What could we women do? For fear of needing to urinate I would not drink water the whole day). I can't help but smile as she relates the reason for her fear. You could have died in the ambush and all you were afraid of was this? I ask incredulously. It is her turn to be surprised. 'Jis zindagi mein hum the usme marne ka dar nahi chalta. Darne ki baat to yeh hai ki jab bathroom jana hai aur ja nahi sakte.' (There is no place for fear of dying in the life I was leading. To be feared is the fact that you cannot relieve yourself when you badly want to go).

The daily camp meeting was held as usual after an 8.00 a.m. breakfast under a tree, the span of its branches providing a natural umbrella. The night before as Kamla lay on her camp bed, which was a mat stretched on the ground, watching the stars above, she had taken a decision which was going to help her get what she wanted now. 'Hum aadmi jaise achcha kaam karte hain toh ek mahila team ko yeh kaam dena chahiye' (our work is as good as the men's so the new operation should be given to an all-women team), she told the group planning the 2008 Battung village ambush. But there was more to her suggestion than the confidence in herself and her women mates. She wanted to show off to her people at home her prowess, gained after joining the Naxal dalaan as a member of the Krantikari Adivasi Sangh (Revolutionary Tribal Group).

Battung was special because it fell in the Narayanpur district where her home was. It had been five years since she had run away from school without telling her parents to go with the Naxals to a training camp in distant Kachchpal in another district. From 2003 to 2006, Kamla travelled forest trails to teach in Naxal camps located in Gadchiroli, north and east Bastar, the largest tribal belt in Chhattisgarh. Besides a few books, Kamla carried a 12-bore gun while on her teaching assignment. When in 2006 she was sent to Abhujmar and posted to the organization's Company No. 1 as a militant in the military wing, she was given a .303 rifle to take part in ambushes. Kamla does not know how many security men she has killed as a member of the Naxal militant wing. 'Team mein sab goli chalate hai. Kiski goli se kaun mara nahin malum. Akhri ginthi se matlab hota hai. Hum bas ginthe hain ki kitne comrade maare gaye.' (Everyone in the team fires. We don't know whose bullet has killed who. We are only interested in the final count of dead. We only count our dead comrades).

Kamla had obviously transited from being a hesitant teenager in Class 5 of Grambasin school, to becoming a dreaded Maoist. She now wore guns. Kamla saw the Battung ambush as an opportunity to let the people she had left behind become aware of this. Her exploits during the ambush would surely be carried soon to her village which was close by. Her mother, father and friends would now learn she had become the fearless deputy commander of a Naxal camp. Could she make this any better? If only she could convince her seniors to give her command of the first ever all-women's Naxal ambush team in the area, she would be admired even more as news of her success in killing security men trickled into Grambasin and the surrounding villages.

The camp leader was fully aware of the daredevil in Kamla. Not only had she proved herself in the Mardapal encounter but also earlier in the 2007 Jharaghati (Narayanpur district) Orchha road encounter which left seven CRPF jawans dead. The Maoists had laid a trap for the security men. The previous day they had executed a police informer. They knew that the police would come to inspect the body. They took positions behind bushes early morning and waited for the police team to arrive. Meanwhile Kamla, risking being spotted in broad daylight, went about for two hours planting bombs on the road the police was expected to use. All she had as protection was a .303 rifle. In a matter of fact voice, Kamla recounts how the team killed all seven policemen who arrived on the spot. But this had become a routine for her. It was the rescue operation of her injured comrade and of the body of another who had died in the encounter that she wants to talk about. In a self-righteous manner she points out that Naxals never leave behind their dead and injured. Every operation has a rescue team standing by a little distance from the scene of action with medicines and stretchers. As the military wing engages in gunfire, others ferry those in need of attention of the rescue team. 'Jaan bachana bhi hamara kaam hai.' (To save lives is our job too).

The irony is lost on Kamla as she talks of the killing of three policemen in the Battung ambush by the all-women team of six she commanded. Armed with an SLR and .303 rifle, she had started the gun battle with thirty policemen. Hours later Grambasin was agog with her exploits.

It was not enough. Kamla wanted something else. She went for it.

*

The garland of flowers weighed heavier than the AK-47 she had wielded all these years. At least that's what Kamla felt that morning in 2008. Two years earlier, in 2006, it was a 12-bore gun she had held for the first time at the Abhujmar Naxal military camp that had set her life on an irreversible path. Now it was to be the marigold garland. It was going to change her life. She was getting married. The moment she exchanged garlands with the man standing opposite her, it would mark a milestone in her life. For a fleeting moment Kamla looked down at her worn-out uniform. She wished for a paata. If she had been at home her mother would have definitely got her one along with flowers to adorn her hair. There may even have been a new silver necklace for the special occasion. But this was a Naxal camp in Kacchapur village, no place for an elaborate wedding. She looked at her comrade Patu whom she had fallen in love with. Her faith in him had grown from the day he, armed with an AK-47 automatic weapon, had stood as a back-up when she led the all-women's team into the Battung encounter. She had relied on him to save her if things got out of hand. She had also chosen him from the many others because he shared her view on continuing in camp even after marriage. In fact he always went along with her decisions. He looked at her and ever so slightly, a move missed by others except Kamla, he extended his garland towards her. Kamla felt she was making the right choice. The two exchanged garlands in the presence of the fifty-odd comrades standing as witness. The wedding ceremony was over. Then it was time to rush to hospital. Her husband had to be sterilized. Having children in a Naxal camp was strictly against the rules. It was rigidly adhered to. Even bachelors went through the procedure to ensure they did not get any woman comrade pregnant.

A couple of months later, Kamla decided to again reshape her life. Marital bliss had been shortlived. They had only a month together in camp. Then he had to return to his platoon. Meetings were sporadic and painfully brief. No, this will not do, Kamla said to herself as she tried to get sleep at the end of a tiring day spent digging trenches. Is this why she had got married? Kamla rolled over on her sleeping mat. Her restlessness had disappeared as it always did when she arrived at a decision. Next morning just after the daily drill Kamla spoke to Arjun, her company chief. Though from Andhra Pradesh he was well acquainted with the culture Kamla came from. She was sure he would accept what she had to say just as he had her choice of husband.

It sounded straight out of a Bollywood script. 'Mujhe maa banna hai....ghar basana hai.' (I want to become a mother... make a home). Arjun had worked with Kamla long enough to know the strength in her decisions. But he had reservations about giving in to her request to permit her to return to her parents in Grambasin. Kamla was high on the wanted list of security agencies. He was sure the police would come for her the moment she left the Naxal camp, which was difficult to detect because they were constantly on the move. They never camped at one spot in the forest for more than a couple of days.

Arjun, like other senior leaders across Naxal camps in

Chhattisgarh, had started to get such requests from battle-hardened women in their cadre. He chose not to question Kamla's decision to leave the organization. Nor was it his place to hold her back. For two months Kamla and her husband were directed to stay in the camp while word was sent to her mother. Kamla returned to her village with her. But her father would not let her stay there. He anticipated the police would soon be at their doorstep to arrest her. She decided to move to the anonymity of a city. Her mother took her to Jagdalpur, the district headquarters.

For the first time in years, Kamla was scared. She lived in fear of the men in khaki, the likes of whom she had fearlessly gunned down many times. In the Kurusnaar (Narayanpur district) encounter she had even killed a high-ranking superintendent of police. But now she was in dread of them. What will happen to me, thought Kamla as she worked on farmland, carried loads and ran errands to earn money. For two years Kamla laboured in the town of Jagdalpur to feed herself and her husband. Should she return to Arjun's camp? No. She yearned for a home, motherhood and a life without fear of getting caught.

Once again Kamla decided to alter the course of her life. She decided to surrender and give up a life on the run. In 2011 she and her husband laid down arms in the presence of government officials and the police. Her son was born a year later. Kamla had what she wanted but was bored sitting at home. Cooking and cleaning and looking after the baby was fine, but she missed action. When the offer came her way, she jumped at it. Not only would it give her money and a status (what is the point in being known only as a former feared Naxalwadi? she comments) but it was a recognition of the skills she had acquired in the Naxal camp.

Now Kamla wears the colours of the Chhattisgarh police.

It has been almost five years since she handed over her gun to the Jagdalpur police and came over-ground. 'Uss din sari-blouse pehne. Shirt-pant khatam.' (That day I wore a sari and blouse. It was an end to the shirt and trousers).

*

Two years after Kamla, Shanti, a girl from another tribal village, followed her into the the dada log camp. By then a new actor had emerged on the Chhattisgarh insurgency theatre._By 2005, Chhattisgarh, which had been in existence for five years as a new state carved out of Madhya Pradesh, was making headlines not only as the hotbed of Naxal insurgency but also for its just-born 'Salwa Judum', a people's militia organized to counter Naxal violence. A year back, in September 2004, the Naxalite movement had taken a different form with the formation of the militant rebel group, CPI (Maoist). This was formed when the People's War Group fused with the Maoist Communist Centre, one of the biggest Maoist groups in India. The Salwa Judum movement was to counter the CPI (M)'s armed wing called the People's Liberation Guerrilla Army (PLGA). In Gondi language, Salwa Judum means purification hunt or peace march. But it was turning out to be the very opposite. The movement started by Mahendra Karma, a Congress MLA of Chhattisgarh in Dantewada district, allegedly with the tacit support of the government, had spread into other Naxal/Maoist insurgency affected districts.

Salwa Judum bands moved from village to village urging people to confront the Naxals. They armed the locals with bows and arrows. Those who refused paid a price. The Salwa Judum movement unleashed its own violence on tribals already under pressure from gun-toting Naxals or Maoists as they were now also called. By the time the Supreme Court of India banned the Salwa Judum movement in July 2011, figures indicated that Salwa Judum men had burned down as many as 644 villages and about 300,000 tribals had to flee their homes. Jangla village in the Bastar district of Chhattisgarh was one of the many caught in the conflict between the Salwa Judum fighters and the rebel Naxals.

Shanti Kunjam, *Member, Krantikari Adivasi Mahila Sangathan (Revolutionary Tribal Women's Organization), Jan Militia (People's Militia)*

It was a frantic dash. All Shanti could hear around her were panic-stricken cries of 'vita, vita' (run, run). She too ran. The entire village was fleeing towards the forest, leaving everything behind. Shanti turned back only once. It was a last longing look at the earthen urn in the hut in which grain was stored. There was no time to pick it up. Jangla village was in danger like hundreds of others of being burnt down by the advancing Salwa Judum militia if its people did not join them.

The people of Jangla had to make a choice. Stay and join the Salwa Judum or flee into the forest and into the bastion of the dada log. They were tragically caught in the crossfire between the Salwa Judum bands and the Naxalites. The Salwa Judum men were pressurizing them to confront the Naxalites. The dada log were urging them to take up guns against the Salwa Judum men or government agents as they were labelled by the Naxals. Both groups were at the doorstep of the cluster of huts that made up the village, both making a bid to recruit the villagers to fight their proxy war. While the leaders of the Salwa Judum movement were knocking on their doors, the Naxals came from the jungle in the dead of night, held meetings and recruited young boys and girls. Leaving behind stored grain, utensils and their meagre possessions, boys, girls and men were running to hide from both gangs in the forest skirting the habitation. Rumours were also milling around about the government sending the Naga battalion from the northeastern state of Nagaland, to the village. This filled them with fear. The Nagas had the reputation in India's heartland of eating human flesh and being ruthless killers. The people of Jangla wanted to escape all three....the Salwa Judum men, the Naxals and the Nagas.

Twenty-two-year-old Shanti also ran, along with the rest of the village folk, into the forest. She did not to want to join either the Salwa Judum or Naxals or take part in the clash between them. Like the others she hid in the forest, not daring to step anywhere near her hut or even her field which she used to till. Wandering in the jungle for two months, braving the rain and scrounging for food, was tough. She was tired and desperate. When the dada log persuaded her to join them she had little choice. For her it meant security. The Naxals had camps in the forest and were getting in touch with all able-bodied boys and girls, motivating them to join their ranks.

These men, wearing army fatigues and armed with guns, were camping in the forest. They moved about and went into villages, urging the locals to fight for their rights over the bounty of the jungle, stand up against the domination of the forest guards and confront the security forces sent in by the government. They promised them freedom from domination by 'outsiders' and control over what rightfully belonged to the tribals, the indigenous people of the Bastar forests. She saw sense in the Naxal view that nature had given the forest people plenty but it was taken away by the government. Shanti liked the empowerment the gun promised. Above all, she enjoyed the songs of rebellion and protest the dadas sang at meetings.

Besides she felt she had little choice but to join them if she wanted to continue living in the forest. There was little for her back home. Her mother had died four years ago when they lived in Kodoli village in Bijapur district. She and her father had then moved to Jangla to his parent's native village. All she did through the day was to tend the little piece of land her father possessed. That too was now gone thanks to the Salwa Judum men.

Shanti joined the Naxals along with a group of fifteen to twenty young people in 2005, six of whom were girls. Along with them she became a member of the Krantikari Adivasi Mahila Sangathan (KMS), the women's wing of the Naxal outfit. The first thing she was made to do was give up her sari for a uniform of trousers and shirt in army colours. For seven months she was trained in the use of arms as they moved camp every one to three days. The camp was always set up at a spot where there was easy access to water. The married women who had joined the dada log were the ones sent to nearby villages to bring back the grain they had stored in their homes. Another method of procuring food and other essentials was to give senior women members Rs 10–15 and they would request locals they knew on their way to the market to shop for them too.

Shanti was on sentry duty at night at her camp. While she kept an eye on suspicious movement as her comrades slept, she had time to herself. Her thoughts always were of her home, her father and brother who had returned to the village. There was plenty she had learnt since she joined the Naxals. Not only did she know how to use a 12-bore gun, deliver motivational speeches at village meetings and make a getaway when the police came in pursuit of them, but also how to give first aid to injured comrades. 'Har platoon mein ek doctor hota hai. Woh operation karke goli nikalta hai, tooti haddi ko plaster karta hai aur bukhaar ki davaee karta hai. Woh sabko yeh sab sikhata bhi hai training mein.' (Every platoon has a doctor. He operates to remove bullets from those injured in combat, puts a caste for broken bones and gives medication for fever. He trains the others for this too).

Her first aid knowledge was tested during a clash with the police when she had gone to address a meeting and distribute pamphlets at Mirthur village near Bhairamgarh. She knew the meeting was a daring assignment as it was to be held very close to the local police post. Shanti was prepared. As the police swooped down on the meeting she along with her mates opened fire. Two of her comrades were injured in the exchange of fire. Santosh, the leader of her group, made sure that the injured were put on the bamboo stretchers they had hidden in the bushes near the venue of the meeting and carried to safety as they ran for cover. Once they were on safe ground, Shanti had to attend to the injured. 'Maine ek lakdi li aur toota huye pair ke saath bandh diya. Doosre ko goli lagi thi. Ghao mein dikh rahi thi. Santosh ney chhuri ko aag mein garam kiya aur maine usse goli ko nikala. Pehle ghao ke dono side par rassi se kas ke baandh liya, khoon rokney ki liye. First aid kit mein davaee thi aur usko bhar diya. Jab doctor ke paas gaye chaar ghante baad usne kaha maine bilkul theek kaam kiya tha.' (I took a branch of a tree and tied it to his broken leg. The other man had a bullet injury. The bullet could be seen embedded in the flesh. Santosh put a knife blade to the fire and with it I scooped out the bullet. But before that I tied a rope at two ends of the wound to prevent excess bleeding. I stuffed the wound with an antiseptic we carried in the first aid kit. After four hours when we saw a doctor he said I had done just the right thing). Shanti keeps her voice low but looks up at me as if waiting for a round of applause for a job done well.

As we sit talking in the one-room home allotted to her as a policewoman, she says she has no regrets about running away from the Salwa Judum men. 'Unke saath bhi maar kaat ka kaam hota. Unke saath khud marne ka chance zaada tha.' (With them too I would have to kill. There were more chances of my being killed if I had gone with them). Salwa Judum founder Mahendra Karma was killed along with twenty-nine other Congress leaders on 25 May 2013 in Darbha Valley, Sukma village, in one of the biggest and most ferocious Naxal ambushes. Years earlier Shanti had assessed that the Maoists were a safer bet than the Salwa Judum.

In fact, Shanti was glad she had joined the Maoists when she heard of the 6 April 2010 assault by them in the jungles of Dantewada district. Said to be one of the deadliest in the history of the Naxal movement in Chhattisgarh, as many as 1,000 Maoists are understood to have taken part.

While Shanti went about doing 'civil' work for her organization, she was always keen to get news about her family. When she went to address village meetings to help build and expand the organization, she often met people from villages close to her own. What they told her was enough to scare her. They told her that her brother, who was now in the police force, was out to hunt her down and kill her for joining the Naxals. But Shanti was keen to return home. She had already been with the Naxals for almost nine years. How long could she escape being killed? 'Militant ki zindagi saath saal se zaada nahi hoti. Mujhe nau saal ho rahe the. Marna toh tha hi, aaj ya kal.' (A militant's life is not more than seven years. I had been one for nine years. I was going to be killed either today or tomorrow). She decided to take her chance.

She took a three-day leave from camp and went to visit her sister in Mopalnar, Dantewada district. While she was there her brother too arrived. But when he learnt that Shanti was there he left without even seeing her. It was her sister who assured her that their brother would not kill her if she wanted to return. That night her brother came quietly to the village. He hid his motorbike some distance away so that its sound would not give him away. He told Shanti that she must realize that she was a terrorist as the CPI (Maoist) had been banned in June 2009 and declared a terrorist group. She actually had little time. The police knew she was in the village and would be coming to arrest her any moment. She had to decide. Did she want to run back to the Naxals or give up the life of a rebel by surrendering to the police? Shanti took a decision on the spot.

She stole into the darkness of the night with her brother. They made it undetected to the hidden motorcycle. Shanti had grown accustomed to movements in the dead of night. It had stopped scaring her. But this was different. She realized that if she was caught she would be shot dead by the police as she was making an escape. She had put her young brother at risk too. He could be killed too or arrested for being her accomplice. She kept her head down as she sped away on his motorbike to a hideout he had arranged. For three days she remained in hiding as her brother worked out the details of her surrender.

On 22 October 2014 Shanti surrendered in Jagdalpur, the headquarters of Bastar district.

Laying down arms or surrender is the only, and very much accepted exit route for Chhattisgarh's women militants. Not only does it guarantee them a safe return home without the police at their heels, frees their families of endless police interrogation (a constant source of worry and distress) but it is the ticket to their ultimate dream...starting their own 'kutumb' (family). This is why a significant number of 'Naxalwadi' women are seen in mass surrenders organized by the government since it intensified anti-terrorist operations from 2010. The largest number was seen in 2015–17.

Many of the Chhattisgarh girls in organized mass surrenders are absolutely unaware of the fact that they have taken part in subversive activity. These are the ones who have never left home for Naxal forest camps. All they have done is collect and store foodgrains for the dada log as asked. They cannot comprehend why they too, like Bhima, Tulsi, Kamla and Shanti are on the wanted list and are being made to surrender. We don't have guns, nor have we killed anyone, they say innocently. Their people agree with them. For that matter they don't hold guilty even those who have. Following the wishes and orders of dada log is a way of life for people in the tribal belt of Chhattisgarh.

NAGALAND

Love and Revolution

'We are also humans...we may be rebels or insurgents or even terrorists as many call us, but we are normal women.'

—*Avuli Chishi Swu*, Executive Member, Steering Committee, NSCN (IM)

SURRENDER MAY BE THE ACCEPTED EXIT ROUTE FOR Chhattisgarh's women militants, but it is a bad word for women militants in the Nagaland insurgency. It is not even considered a choice or a decision an individual can take at a personal level. To parley with the government, talk peace and lay down arms are decisions taken by the militant organization's top leadership as in the case of the National Socialist Council of Nagalim (Isak-Muivah). The women in the NSCN (IM) have little to do with arms now but they continue to work for the government-in-exile (Government of the People's Republic of Nagaland) formed in 1980 with the birth of the NSCN, the forerunner of which was the Naga National Council (NNC). The NNC fragmented when its senior members Thuingaleng Muivah, Isak Swu and S.S. Khaplang opposed the Shillong Accord other NNC leaders had inked with the Indian government and set up the NSCN.

Eight years later (1988), Muivah, Isak Swu and S.S. Khaplang fell out over continuation of the 1997 Ceasefire Agreement with the Government of India and split the NSCN into the Isak-Muivah (IM) and Khaplang (K) factions. Khaplang opted out of the Ceasefire Agreement and moved to a camp in Myanmar where he died on 9 June 2017. In fact, as the NNC began to peter out and Phizo died in London in 1991, the NSCN (IM) faction came to be considered as the mother of all insurgencies in India's troubled northeast region, patronizing other smaller extremist outfits where Naga tribes live, like the hill districts of Manipur, Assam and Arunachal Pradesh. The NSCN (IM) influence stretches even to the northwestern part of Myanmar which also has the presence of Naga tribes. There are about sixty-nine Naga tribes in all the northeastern states of India and Myanmar. Seventeen tribes alone live in Nagaland. However, in the Naga areas of Myanmar it is the NSCN (K) group which is the main force. The NSCN (IM) was banned by the Indian government in November 1990.

When Muivah and Khaplang parted ways they divided the areas where the writ of the GPRN (Government of the People's Republic of Nagaland) of each faction would run. Since then the NSCN (IM) runs a parallel government from the Hebron designated camp some 45 kms from Dimapur with founder Muivah as the prime minister. About 6,000 NSCN (IM) cadre work on a stipend in its civil and military wing. The military training camp in Lilen village holds a passing out parade of about 200 people three to four times a year. It regularly recruits people for the its Naga Civil Service. Its chief administrative officers are drawn from here and are responsible for disposal of cases of dispute and conflict between the many Naga tribes as well as tax collection. The NSCN (IM) women cadre who were underground before the ceasefire continue to work for the GPRN.

The women militants in Nagaland never sever links with the organization they join. The reason for it is their absolute commitment to the ideology, for the sake of which they join the ranks of militant groups in the first place, and give it their all. Mostly educated, they step into insurgent groups after much deliberation, driven by their belief that the cause they are taking up the gun for is just and right. The cause remains first in their lives. Men in Nagaland, even those not involved in insurgency, are proud of their women militants. They command a special respect in their society. Since women in Nagaland's social milieu have never been seen as inferior or subordinate, their leaving a home environment for years to fight alongside men is not an issue. When they return they are hailed as the brave ones and their dedication much appreciated. Their work and sacrifice for the cause is recognized by leaders as in the case of Avuli Chishi Swu who was amongst the first lot of women militants to go to China in 1974, to procure arms and for arms training. Now she is an executive member of the NSCN (IM) Steering Committee and amongst the top three leaders of her organization.

Avuli Chishi Swu

Six decades ago, Avuli was just a frightened child watching soldiers of the Indian Army set her village on fire. Her dark eyes reflected a dance of fiery orange ribbons. The nine-year-old girl stood trembling, hiding behind a tree. Tears intermittently blurred the orange streaks but Avuli Chishi Swu made no attempt to wipe the salty rivulets running down her cheeks. She just watched, helpless as many times before, stifling her sobs so that they would not give away her sanctuary. Not that she could be heard in the mayhem around and nor did anyone have time for a scared little girl. Shesulimi village in Nagaland, a state in India's extreme northeast, was on fire. The flames soared, licked and finally swallowed the thatched wooden huts in the village, home to the Sumi tribe, also called Sema, one of the largest of the seventeen main ones that inhabit the state which shares a border with Myanmar on its east. This was the ninth time during the year 1963–64 that the Indian Army had set ablaze her dwelling to crush the ongoing Naga rebellion to secede from India, spearheaded by the Naga National Council under the stewardship of its militant leader, Angami Zapu Phizo.

As far back as she could remember she had seen Indian soldiers raid her village, burn it down, beat up people and even take them away, sometimes never to return. Little Avuli could not comprehend the frequent assaults by army men and the reasons for it. All she knew was that when the soldiers came they brought violence that left her frightened and crying. Unknown to her, the traumatic events that were to shape her life had been set in motion even before she was born. The confrontation between Indian soldiers and the Nagas was the fallout of Phizo turning the NNC into an armed struggle some decades ago.

The Naga resistance, not militant to start with, dates back to 1918 with the formation of the Naga Club. In 1929, its leaders told the Simon Commission (sent by the British to India to see the progress of the governance of its colony and which later suggested provincial autonomy as a Constitutional reform) 'to leave us alone to determine for ourselves as in ancient times'. In 1946, the Club was recognized as a political organization and took on the name of the Naga National Council (NNC). On 14 August 1947, on the eve of India's independence, Phizo, the third NNC chairman, declared Nagaland an independent state and resolved to establish a 'sovereign Naga state'. In 1951, it conducted a 'referendum' in the Naga state in which '99 per cent' supported an 'independent' Nagaland.

On 22 March 1952, Phizo formed the underground Naga Federal Government (NFG) and the Naga Federal Army (NFA). The Government of India sent in its army to crush the insurgency. In 1954, Phizo went on to form the 'People's Sovereign Republic of Free Nagaland'. In January 1956, the Indian government declared the Nagaland Hill District a 'Disturbed Area' and put it under army control. Later in the year Phizo escaped to London. In 1958, India's Central Government enacted the Armed Forces Special Powers Act (AFSPA) and deployed its army to smother the long-running Naga insurgency.

In December 1963, Nagaland became another state of India. Underground rebel groups continued their armed struggle for secession from India. Though there was a decline in the movement for independence, the men from the military wing of the NNC encountered Indian soldiers undertaking counter-insurgency operations. The operations became more intense when the NNC refused to honour the April 1964 agreement some of its leaders signed with the Government of India to suspend its operations and talk peace. Finally, the government banned the NNC in 1967 under the Unlawful Activities Prevention Act.

The soldiers came to Avuli's village in 1964 as part of the massive counter-insurgency operation. They were more ruthless than before. The army's mandate was to wipe out the NNC, NFG and NFA militants continuing the armed resistance in violation of the just-inked agreement to suspend operations and work out a peaceful solution. During the army raids Avuli's home and parents were special targets. Her mother, Khuli Swu, was marked because she was the chairperson of the women's wing of the NNC. Once earlier she had been whisked away by army men when her son was only five days old. For six days no one in the village knew where she and the newborn were. Avuli had cried, then too feeling helpless, as she waited for their return. She cried again when her father, Khakhu Swu, was dragged out by soldiers during a raid and beaten with the butt of a gun. Again she was overcome by a sense of helplessness. As the little girl stood behind the tree and looked at her burning house, she made a resolve. She was going to put an end to being powerless in front of Indian soldiers.

Ten years later, nineteen-year-old Avuli lived up to her resolve. The date, like all other important ones in her life, is etched in her mind. Her age of sixty has not blunted her ability to recall dates in a jiffy. Like a computer she comes up with the precise date and year. 'It was 21 September 1974 when I joined the Naga Army (military wing of the NNC) to fight the Indian State. I was a nineteen-year-old schoolgirl studying in Pughoboto. The atrocities by the Indian soldiers which I had seen as a child left indelible scars on my mind. I had resolved at that time that I would fight them when I was older.'

Alleged atrocities during anti-insurgency operations by Indian soldiers is seen as the single factor in motivating Naga women to break from their tradition of never participating in armed combat. The Nagas have a strong warrior tradition in which territorial wars and inter-tribal clashes had been bloody and frequent. But fighting was always left to the men. It is another matter that Naga women in times gone by judged a man's bravery and courage by the number of scalps of enemies he carried as trophies. Headhunters never had a dearth of brides. In a culture where fierce battles for one's tribe and village territory were fought with spears and bows and arrows, the traditional role of women was to bring them to an end when the violence and killing went beyond a point. Armed with forked wooden staves, they would enter the battlefield and use the poles to separate the fighting men. They did not ever touch the men nor were the men allowed to touch them. But they had to cease the fight once the women disengaged them.

The Naga women stepped out of their role as conflict mediators, wives, house managers, food providers and child-bearers when they saw their brave men being beaten up and wounded by gun-bearing soldiers. The NNC found them willing recruits to fight the Indian Army. Avuli remembers her mother being so involved with the NNC that she had 'no time to cook or take care of her children'. But it did not bother Avuli. In fact her mother was a big influence in her resolve to join the Naga army when she grew up.

The determination to live up to her resolution with no regrets about whatever it may take to do so, is evident in her 49-year journey from a young recruit to becoming the third seniormost in the hierarchy of the Nationalist Socialist Council of Nagalim (IM).

*

For Avuli the biggest test of her determination and resolve to fight the Indian Army soldiers for the Naga cause was her eight-month trek to China in the December of 1974. 'On 6 December 1974, I exchanged my lotosu and chakutha qhumu (traditional handwoven cloth tied at the waist as a straight ankle-length skirt and shawl worn by the Sumi women) for jungle fatigues.' Avuli became a member of the historic second batch of the NNC led by a Phizo confidant to go to China for arms training and join the first batch, which had been taken there by Thuingaleng Muivah, another close aide of Phizo. 'We were twenty women in a group of 375 men led by Isak Chishi Swu, who later became head of the NSCN (IM) faction along with Muivah. Only twelve of us reached China. Of them four were women. All others perished during the journey.' Isak's wife along with eight other women had gone earlier to the China camp in the first NNC batch.

The worst part of the journey, recalls Avuli, was when she had her monthly period. None of the women had come prepared for the journey that took several months. 'We trudged with blood on our legs and stained uniforms. I salute my men comrades who ignored the telltale patches, pretending they had not seen the bloodstains to save us embarrassment.' Avuli was not going to give in to feeling helpless in this situation. She found a way to mitigate the mortification and discomfort. 'As soon as I saw a waterfall I would rush to stand under it or sit in the river so that the water could wash off the blood. I have no regrets that I had to undergo this ignominy. Nothing mattered to me. All I wanted was to reach China.'

The Naga rebels were the first to go to China looking for aid. They were sent by Phizo to China via Myanmar to seek support, military training and arms. But it was a gruelling journey on foot. They did not have any arms to fight the Indian and Burmese armies that were hunting them. Sometimes they were attacked by the non-Naga tribesmen of Myanmar. Avuli recalls the experience as one that taught her to live without food and water for long stretches. More important for her were lessons learnt on how to come to terms with death and loss of loved ones. 'We had to take a circuitous route to avoid the Indian Army as well as the Burmese army. Once I had to go without food for twenty-five days. Water was also scarce unless we found a flowing stream which would give us clean water.' But she does not make much of it, mentioning it only in passing.

What she wants to talk about is the death of two of the girls who had become her friends during the journey. She lost a friend first near the Chindwin river in Myanmar as they marched towards the China camp. Avuli and her comrade were holding hands to support each other as they made their way through dense foliage and treacherous terrain. They were ambushed by Burmese soldiers who were so close that they could touch them. 'I saw my friend fall to the ground as a bayonet pierced her head.' The group scattered and each one ran for cover. 'I had to run. I could not even turn to see if she was dead or just injured. I had to leave her.' Avuli's impassive face undergoes a change. Her unlined forehead suddenly becomes creased with wrinkles. It is easy to realize that she is reliving the painful moment when she had to abandon her friend and was unable to go to her aid. It was only after five days that they regrouped.

There could be no turning back to look for her friend. Avuli did not know how to bear her loss and reconcile to the guilt of deserting her friend. She decided to do what she was good at and something that would bring about a closure. 'I wove a shawl in her memory and left it there,' she says wistfully. Tears threaten her eyes. I know she has vowed not to cry. The silence that follows speaks volumes of her struggle to stick to her pledge. I try to help.

I reach out to hold her hand to comfort her. Avuli makes a move that takes me completely by surprise. She takes off her black and red shawl and drapes it across my shoulder. The gesture is so sentimental and in total contrast to the emotionless persona she has projected to me so far. A shawl is full of significance for Nagas. Woven only by women, it reveals the hierarchy of the wearer in society, her status and the tribe she comes from. By giving me her shawl, what was Avuli, a person of few words, trying to tell me? Was she expressing thanks for my understanding her pain or was she accepting me as a friend? Whatever it may be, from that moment it was Avuli revealed. All the violence she has lived though has not been able to harden her soft core.

Now her conversation began to be interspersed with her feelings about the facts she was relating. 'Just see the irony of it all. I lost another friend just when we had almost reached our final destination. She was washed away by the fast currents of the Chindwin river just when we crossed it and entered China. She was so close to her destination and yet could not make it. This made me believe that God let me survive because he had a purpose for me. That is why He put me in this situation.'

It was with a renewed sense of purpose that she started her military training on arrival at the Chinese training camp. 'We reached the Kutungn training centre in China on 14 August

1975. I think it was in Kunming province. Our journey on foot from the Naga Hills to China via Kachin in Myanmar had taken eight months but our enthusiasm had not waned even though we had seen death at close quarters and faced disease, thirst and hunger. I just wanted to learn how to use the gun and achieve my goal.' Avuli and the other three women trained with the men to use M-29 guns, light machine guns, semi-automatic rifles, make bombs and the Improvised Explosive Device which the NNC was later known to often use as roadside bombs when it ambushed Indian troops.

The evening entertainment at the camp was to tune in to All India Radio to keep abreast with happenings in India. It was one such evening, barely three months since their arrival in China, when they heard the news that is a watershed in the history of the Naga insurgency movement. It personally affected Avuli, now a trained member in the army wing of the NNC, and her comrades. On 11 November 1975, a section of NNC leaders had signed the Shillong Accord, under which the NNC and NFG agreed to give up arms. It stunned the NNC group training in China. Avuli and her group led by Thuingaleng Muivah, along with seniors Isak and S.S. Khaplang who were at that time with them, condemned the Accord, called it a betrayal and refused to accept it.

Unknown to Avuli, the leaders were planning how to keep the NNC afloat to fight for secession from India. 'In February 1976 we returned to Eastern Nagaland (Myanmar) to the NNC General Headquarters (GHQ) in Chon village. We carried arms and ammunition we had bought in China.' Avuli was appointed section commander of the Women's Wing of the NNC. There were about twenty-five women who were trained to climb trees and scale mountains. Special medical training was given to the women. 'Women were kept as the second line of defence in bunkers while the men were in the forefront during encounters and ambushes. The role of women was clearly defined. We would give them first aid when they were injured.' However, the arms training imparted was the same for men and women cadres. In 1978 there were 100 female staffers in GHQ.[16]

She had spent barely six months in the GHQ when there was a need to get another consignment of arms from China. Avuli was the first amongst the three women to volunteer to go. 'Along with some men we left Phulong Tong camp on 12 September 1976 for the Kutungn training camp in China.' The return journey become tougher because of the load of arms and ammunition she had to carry in a rucksack on her back. The risky and arduous treks to ferry arms do not seem to have bothered her. For Avuli it was a must-do to achieve their goal. Besides these were shorter trips compared to the first one to China. 'I was also well trained by now.' Avuli brushes away talk of the difficulties saying 'nothing mattered except the fact that I was working to achieve my goal.'

On her return Avuli was promoted to the rank of sergeant. She saw plenty of action while serving in the military wing. While the women were not sent into operations or to lay an ambush, they joined the patrol groups guarding the camps. 'But I dreamt of going for an ambush.' Only once did she get a chance to be part of an ambush squad and that too only as a substitute. Avuli was ambushed by soldiers eight times. Five times it was in Nagaland itself, twice in Myanmar near the Chindwin river, once on the banks of the Irrawaddy river and once at Tangkho village in Myanmar. 'It was in March 1977 that the Burmese Lenung tribesmen attacked the Naga camp in

---

16. Phanjoubam Tarapot, *Insurgency Movement in Northeastern India*, p. 112, Vikas Publishing House, New Delhi, 1993.

Tangkho. The ambush began at 4.00 a.m. and lasted till noon.' Once again Avuli escaped death when a two-inch mortar fell near her, rendering her deaf in the left ear for two months. After all these years she still hears a ringing in her ear.

Sometime between firing guns, making bombs and defying death, Avuli fell in love. Nihokhe Swu was a major in the Naga army. 'When you work together and face danger together it is easy to fall in love. It builds a strong bond that pulls you towards each other,' is Avuli's rather pragmatic analysis of how love can spring up in a violence-ridden environment. After permission was granted by their leaders 'we married on 22 December 1978 in a simple Christian ceremony at camp.' There was no flowing white gown or flowers. 'I was in my army uniform.' In the presence of camp mates, the camp chaplain instructed them to exchange vows. A simple feast followed. Barely does she finish relating this when in the same breath Avuli talks of her husband's death. 'On 21 January1980 he was killed in a clash with the Burmese army.' She utters it like reading an official statement. The emotional quotient in her voice is introduced surprisingly only when she gives the next significant date in her life. 'On 30 January 1980, Isak, Muivah and Khaplang formed the National Socialist Council of Nagalim (NSCN) to continue the armed struggle.'

Avuli was in detention in Thingningan village in Myanmar when the NSCN was formed. While posted in the village she was unfortunately tracked down by the NNC faction that had signed the Shillong Accord. She was confined by them for five months for being from the anti-Accord group. But she remained determined in her resolve to fight the Indian Army. On her release, when she learnt that Muivah, Isak and Khaplang had left the NNC and formed the NSCN, she decided to return to them. She travelled to the NSCN Operational GHQ in

Tayongngan village on the Kachin–China border and rejoined the Naga army. The rebels had started to set up bases in areas where Naga tribes live. For five days she stayed at the GHQ and was later escorted (it was the practice for the men to accompany women comrades when they were shifted from one place to another), to the NSCN Central Headquarters (CHQ) in camp Tonu in Myanmar. Here she met Isak and Muivah. 'I was very excited at meeting my senior leaders and working with them.' Here Avuli was promoted to the rank of sergeant major.

While Avuli focused on the use of arms, a junior militant in the camp trained his eyes on her. She had not the faintest idea that Qhevihe Chishi Swu (now convenor of the Steering Committee of the NSCN-IM faction) was fascinated by her. 'I did not want to remarry but he pursued me. He is my late husband's cousin and my family too wanted me to remarry. As I said when you work together you establish a strong bond. I married him in March 1983 because of this bond. The more dangers we faced together the more we fell in love. I realized how much our love had become stronger when he was jailed in Jodhpur in Rajasthan for a year in 1996 and we had to live apart.' After her marriage to Qhevihe she moved from the military wing to the civil wing of NSCN. A year later she became the vice-chairman of the women's wing (National Socialist Women's Organization of Nagalim).

The tough life in the camp took its toll on Avuli's two sons. Malaria was not easy to beat at the camp located in a clearing in thick forest. Mosquito repellents proved inadequate for babies still to build immunity. Lack of clean potable water often led to typhoid. 'My sons fell very sick. I decided to take them to Dimapur in Nagaland for treatment.' When I ask how old they were, Avuli most uncharacteristically cannot recall the dates when they were born. 'I think the elder one was about three years and younger one was just about one and a half.' But she remembers the exact day when the NSCN went through a calamity that threatened its future existence. 'While on the way from the camp in Myanmar to Nagaland, I got the news that on 30 April 1988, the NSCN had split into NSCN (IM) and NSCN (K). There was a bloody crisis when Isak and Muivah had differences with Khaplang. Isak and Muivah together formed the NSCN (IM) and Khaplang formed the NSCN (K).' Avuli chose to remain with NSCN (IM). 'Isak was from the same tribe as mine.'

The split was marked by inter-factional killings with allegations that Khaplang executed as many as 100 of Isak's men when he attacked the Hanseng camp (Myanmar) where the supporters of Muivah and Isak were meeting. Isak himself escaped an attempt on his life. The event is considered one of the bloodiest in the Naga history. On 30 April 1988, Khaplang's men and the Burmese troops encircled and attacked the NSCN Central Headquarters. Of the 230 NSCN (IM) cadres who survived, most were women and children.[17]

In 1991, Avuli, who was in Dimapur nursing her sons who were recovering from malaria and typhoid, was assigned to mobilize people for the outlawed NSCN (IM). As always she did not allow anything, including motherhood, to stand in the way of her work for the organization. She strapped her six-month-old baby daughter to her back, held her two little sons by their hands and walked from village to village addressing meetings, spreading the NSCN (IM) message and recruiting people for the cause. Walking was the safest if not the easiest way of reaching people in scattered villages. A woman trudging

---

17. Phanjoubam Tarapot, *Insurgency Movement in Northeastern India*, p. 123.

with her children in tow did not look a likely rebel and those on the lookout for one were fooled. 'I was pregnant too, so I hardly raised the suspicion of the soldiers and police.' As she walked past police posts and barricades none realized that she was the chairman of the women's wing of the NSCN (IM), by then the most active insurgent group in the area fighting for the Naga cause.

In 1992, NSCN (IM) set up a GHQ at Yangkhunao in Manipur near its border with Nagaland. This was the first on Indian soil. The camp consisted of fifty-two huts in which about 100 cadres, including women, lived. It was the nerve centre from where its commander-in-chief issued orders, carried out recruitment and training.[18] The largest military camps of the NSCN (IM) were located in Myanmar. There were many women like Avuli more than enthusiastic to join the NSCN (IM) and work for the Naga cause. Avuli was obviously amongst the very first few to do so.

Did she not think that having children would stand in the way of her work? 'No, I did not let that happen. I raised five children, three girls and two boys, and also worked for the cause. It has meant my life to me.' In those violent troubled days when there was no surety of life, how could you manage having children and that too five? I ask. How did you find time to indulge in romantic moments in the midst of such turbulence? Avuli's face sheds its severe look and she clasps my hand with both of hers. 'We are also humans,' she says somberly. 'I want you to understand that we may be rebels or insurgents or even terrorists as many call us, but we are normal women.' She pats the shawl she had given me earlier, woven and worn

18. Phanjoubam Tarapot, *Insurgency Movement in Northeastern India*, p. 130.

only by women, and says, 'This is to remember me as a normal woman...a woman who sees in you another who can understand that love and fighting for a cause can go together because you fight for something you love.' Naga women ordinarily love peace, she adds, but 'we have not lived in ordinary times for decades.'

Theimila Shimray

If times had been any different, teenager Theimila Shimray, barely five feet three inches in height, slim, fair, her ready smile made even more captivating by two deep dimples on her cheeks, would have had much more to fascinate her than stories about the armed struggle for Naga independence. Admiring glances from men usually followed her as she walked past and in more peaceful times, she could have lived the life of a village belle.

The year 1987 was no ordinary time for the Naga people—men and women, young and old. It was normal for young girls to cherish the cause for an exclusive independent Naga homeland where Naga tribes, not only in Nagaland but the contiguous adjoining states of Manipur, Assam and Arunachal Pradesh and even across the border in Myanmar, could live. To join underground organizations to fight for this was the normal in those days. This is exactly what Theimila Shimray did when she turned twenty. On 16 February 1987, she enlisted for the outlawed Naga army. Theimila of the Tangkhul Naga tribe, living in the predominantly Naga Ukhrul district of Manipur, was motivated by her friend, already a member of the NSCN, to go for military training to a camp in east Nagaland (Myanmar). 'My friend had often spoken about the brave people in Nagaland fighting for Greater Nagaland. I knew about them and admired what they were doing.' This was reason enough for her to decide to join the NSCN.

It was a group of thirty, including ten girls, which set out by bus from the nearby village of Langdang for the NSCN military training camp in the jungles on the border with Myanmar. 'I was very excited. The initial journey was easy.' Their first stop was the Khangkhui NSCN camp near the Ukhrul district itself. After a three-day stay there, the group took another bus for Dimapur in Nagaland. The next day they travelled to Digit town. From there began the difficult part of the journey.

It was a tough five-day trek to Tonu camp in eastern Nagaland. 'I experienced hunger for the first time in my life,' says Theimila. Her infectious ready smile belies the discomfort of it all. 'Our next meal depended on the reaction of the people in the village we stopped at. Sometimes they would shout at us and shoo us away. At times they would give us some rice or maize or tapioca. We had to live on what they handed out to us. There were no shops we could buy food from.' Unknown to Theimila and her companions, this was a taste of things to come.

When they reached Tonu camp, Theimila saw it was no paradise. But it did not deter her from life as a rebel. The camp was a clearing in a forest in which stood a cluster of bamboo huts thatched with leaves and plastic sheets. Procuring rations was not easy. 'We had to go to nearby villages and indent rations. Sometimes we requested and sometimes intimidated the villagers when they refused to part with rice.'

Theimila's military training lasted till 1 May 1987. From 6.00 a.m. to 10.30 a.m. they were made to do physical exercises, target practice, rope climbing and learn the use of guns. 'More than anything else the training taught us discipline and gave us a feeling of power. I felt I could do anything. I also developed more emotional strength. I was never one to be afraid, but now I began to feel that nothing could be scary...except the Burmese army. They could attack the camp any time.'

Theimila however refused to cave in to the fear of an attack. Instead, she looked forward to the evenings at Tonu camp. They were full of fun for her. 'In the evenings we played volleyball, badminton or football.' Volleyball and football matches were between the NSCN team and teams of other organizations that had camps in the same complex. The Tonu camp space was shared by other insurgent outfits of the northeast like the United National Liberation Front (UNLF), the oldest insurgent group of Manipur, the People's Liberation Army of Manipur (PLA) and the United Liberation Front of Asom (ULFA) of Assam.

Football is encouraged and played at most insurgent camps in the northeast probably because it is a favourite of well-known leaders like Paresh Baruah, chief of ULFA's military wing and S.S. Khaplang who later became chief of a splinter faction of the NSCN. Baruah, in his student days, was selected for the Assam football team and played many tournaments. Inter-organization football matches were organized in camps to celebrate the ULFA Raising Day, Christmas and Assam's Bihu festival with Baruah part of the team and Khaplang a special invitee.[19] 'I like to win and enjoyed defeating the rival teams,' Theimilla told me with a smug smile. Few realized that the petite and ever-smiling rebel played every evening only for a win. Her extrovert nature hid her steely determination to succeed in everything she undertook. For her a match was an exercise in learning how to assess the strength of the rival, identify his weakness and accordingly devise a strategy to defeat him. 'Winning matches gave me confidence in myself. Matches were a test of my willpower and determination to overcome obstacles and attain my goal.' It was only in the sports field that the cadres competed with

19. Rajeev Bhattacharya, *Rendezvous with Rebels*, pp. 126, 212, HarperCollins *Publishers* India, 2014.

each other. At times they trained together, worked together and together made forays into nearby settlements for food. 'We could be identified only by the colour of our uniform. Each organization had a different shade of green for its uniform.'

After she was done with her training, Theimila took an examination that qualified her to become an accountant. 'I joined the Nationalist Socialist Women's wing of Nagalim (NSWON) in May 1987 and worked in the NSCN Council Headquarters in the Hangsen Camp (Myanmar) till it was attacked by Khaplang's men on 30 April 1988.' Early that morning, when Theimila rose for her bath, she had no idea that it was a date which was going to assume historical significance for the NSCN. 'It was still dark when I went to the toilet at 4.30 a.m. Suddenly I heard gunshots and people in the mess shouting to us to run.' Theimila, however, could not think of leaving behind her accounts register. She ran to her room, collected her accounts book and a few essentials kept ready in a kit in the eventuality of an attack by the Burmese army, and sped towards the forest skirting the camp. 'We were six or seven of us. It took us about half hour to reach the mountains bordering the forest. We hid there.'

Theimila could see the smoke rising from the camp destroyed by Khaplang's men. They were joined by the Burmese soldiers who 'threw bombs into the camp area'. As they were fleeing, they saw their comrades being killed by men from the Khaplang faction. She was aware that the NSCN had split and these men, some of whom she had worked with earlier, were now hunting them down. 'When we reassembled in the forest we were fifteen of us. Only two were men. I was told that thirty of our comrades had been killed as we were running away.' Concealing themselves in the thick forest and mountains was not too difficult. 'We had to make sure we cooked when it was still light so the flame could not be spotted.'

Theimila had more to worry about than cooking the rice and maize which was fast running out. 'The forest was full of earthworms and leeches. They came through my trousers and stuck to my legs. I knew a leech was sucking my blood only when it would start paining and itching.' She would run behind a tree or bush, take off her clothes, sprinkle salt on the affected area and pull the leech out with the help of a leaf. 'I saved all the salt I could for this instead of putting it in my food.'

After a fortnight of hiding, Theimila and her friends came across a rivulet. It had been days since they had had a wash. 'Even on the day of the attack I had not finished my bath when I had to run. When we saw the river we were tempted.' The bath turned out to be a security lapse. Men from the rival faction were searching for those who had escaped the attack on the Hangsen camp. 'We were bathing in a river when we were captured.' It was 15 May 1988. This was a situation in which Theimila knew she could not win. 'They were armed. We had left our clothes and weapons on the river bank and we were in the water.' Khaplang's men meant business. Theimila and her companions knew the futility of offering any resistance.

They were marched to the NSCN (K) camp in Taga. 'We were interrogated for ten days. They were actually looking for senior NSCN (IM) leaders. When they realized we were very junior, they asked us for information on what was going on in the Hangsen camp before the attack.' Much to Theimila's despair they 'tore up my accounts book'. But its loss paled when she saw the two boys in her group killed by Khaplang's men. She started to wonder what awaited her and the other girls. After ten days they were taken to a village and confined there. 'The living conditions were terrible. The place was full of mosquitoes and no medical aid was available to us. Some of the girls died of malaria fever.' But Theimila told herself that she must stay alive. 'I did not want to die—at least not in the enemy camp. It is another thing to die in battle than dying in captivity.' Through the day she kept motivating herself. 'I kept telling myself that I had to live and somehow get out of this.' Soon the girls were moved again.

It took two months of trekking through forests and over mountains to reach the Wanruk camp on the Myanmar border. Here they were taken to Khaplang, the leader of their captors. When she first saw him she was surprised. 'He was known as a ruthless man. But he was thin with a slight hump. He looked weak and ill. It was said that he took opium though it was banned in his camp. He lived and behaved like an Angh (chief of a Naga village). There were no rules for him,' recalls Theimila. (Khaplang died in June 2017 at his camp in the Kachin State of Myanmar). Not one to be in awe of anyone, even the known leader of a rival insurgent group, she took the meeting in her stride. The only thought in her mind was how she was going to flee Wanruk.

Khaplang had been told by his men who had interrogated Theimila that she was an experienced accountant and proficient at administrative work. 'He asked me to work as his personal secretary in his office. I had no choice but to agree.' Was she afraid? 'No, not at all. If he did anything to me I could have given him one hit. He was so frail.' But young Theimila had another strategy.' I decided I would win his respect by being good at my work.' She attended to his correspondence, kept books and records for him. 'He always praised my work.' She was also asked to put in hours in the office of the NSCN (K) women's wing which had about 'forty or fifty members.'

All the while Theimila kept her eyes and ears open and stayed alert to things around. 'People whispered all sorts of things about Khaplang though he was their leader. But I did not indulge in gossip because I knew it could be dangerous for me. If I said anything negative about him they would carry it to him and I would lose his confidence.' The biggest scandal in the camp was when an unmarried girl who did chores in Khaplang's quarters became pregnant. Within days of the discovery she disappeared. 'No one knew where she was sent off or what happened to her. The camp rules were very strict and the man responsible would ordinarily have been taken to task. In this case there was no inquiry and no one was punished. This led to a lot of gossip and finger-pointing.'

The damp climate in the Wanruk camp made Theimila sick. She was afflicted by chronic cold and developed asthma. 'I used this as an excuse with Khaplang to escape his camp.' She asked for leave to go to Digit for treatment. He agreed to let her go. It was October 1989. 'I was accompanied by six others and we walked all the way to Digit. From there I hired a taxi and drove to Dimapur never to return to Khaplang.' From Dimapur, Theimila made her way to the NSCN (IM) Council Headquarters in Senapati district of Manipur. 'I was happy to be back but even more happy that I could now continue work for my group [NSCN(IM)].' She was appointed office assistant here. There was another reason that made her return even happier. It had taken her past the Loyi checkpost and once again she had met the handsome Dhungshin from the organization's military wing.

Theimila had not forgotten her first meeting with him when as a fresh recruit she was on her way from the Khangkhui camp to the Tonu camp. 'I was attracted to him. He was a corporal. He is not very tall, only five feet six inches, but I am only five feet three inches so I found him tall and dashing. I like men in uniform or rather, found the Naga army uniform very appealing. I had just got mine.' She may have liked the military fatigues but soon realized that 'I preferred office work and being on the civilian side more than being in the military wing. Not that I was afraid of action but I felt that I could use my skills better in the civilian side.' Being a meticulous person, she likes maintaining files and records. In 1990 she was promoted as a section officer in the office of Appeals in the Sorbung camp.

Life at the Sorbung camp took on a new meaning for Theimila when Dhungshin was also posted there. Not only was the work of attending to complaints and appeals and finding ways to redress them interesting for her, but she found in Dhungshin a man who 'cared for me'. When existence is threatened by violence ever so often and the rigour of camp life makes each day tough going, 'even the smallest gesture of help means a lot'. Theimila always found Dhungshin by her side when she was ill. He came to her aid when she craved sweets and eggs not often available in the camp mess. 'He would always give me money to go to the nearby shops and buy sweets. He knew I love eggs and would tell me to go and buy them when the mess ran out of them.'

When she moved to the Thingva camp a few months later she was overjoyed to know that Dhungshin was also being sent there. Friendship and a strong attraction for each other led to a more intense emotion. 'I realized how much he cared for me and loved me the day the camp was attacked by the Indian Army.' Characteristically, Theimila thought of saving the files and records instead of running for cover. 'I gathered them and shifted them out of the building before it was destroyed.' To help her was none other than Dhungshin. She is puzzled at my view that falling in love is difficult in violent times. 'What has violence got to do with falling in love?' she asks. 'Who cares what is happening around when one is falling in love? Falling in love is easier in uncertain times.' NSCN(IM)'s Section Officer

Theilima and Sergeant Major Dhungshin Shimray decided to marry. They married in Dimapur in January 1992, as soon as they were granted the mandatory permission from their leaders. A church wedding and traditional festivities had to be given a pass because of the prevailing situation. It would have attracted too much attention of security and intelligence men. Later, the devout Christian that she is, Theilima cleared her conscience. 'I went to church and confessed to the priest that I had married.'

The newlyweds could not stay together in Dimapur for long. Theimila had opted out of camp life but her husband had to go out on postings. It was a disturbed married life 'but I knew that the work of the NSCN (IM) had to go on'. Theimila had become a mother and spent time looking after the children. It was only after the NSCN (IM) signed the Ceasefire Agreement with the Government of India in August 1997, that Theimila could set up a proper home and live a normal married life. While Dhungshin is now a member of the NSCN (IM) Steering Committee, Theimila is secretary of the NSWON. She echoes what her senior Avuli Chishi Swu had told me. 'We women like peace and we want it. We have seen enough of violence and were part of it only because of the cause of Nagaland.' Since Muivah signed the historic Peace Accord with the Indian government on August 2015, she, along with Avuli, has been hoping for a lasting peace. They now work on the welfare schemes for women in the GPRN. In times of violence women suffer the most. So it is the women who have to fight for peace again just as 'the Naga women traditionally have,' says Avuli. For her and Theimila there have already been enough killings. A peaceful solution has to be found to meet the Naga aspirations. That is what their fight is for now.

Avuli and Theimila, like the rest of the NSCN (IM), are closely following the progress on the 2015 Framework

Agreement signed in the presence of Prime Minister Narendra Modi to set the agenda for formulating a final solution to the vexed Naga problem. Other Naga political groups along with the NSCN (IM) are at the conference table. The main hurdle is the demand for the creation of Greater Nagaland (Nagalim), which will include Naga-inhabited areas in other states of northeastern India and even northern Myanmar. As of now the government has ruled this out. As a compromise, it is ready to agree to whatever else will protect the Naga identity and culture, a solution that has so far not worked out. A wistful Avuli points out that peace is taking its time to come to her homeland.

ASSAM

Flames of the Forest

'I always kept my cheek with the dimple towards the other passengers in the bus when I was transporting arms. I use my smile as a weapon.'

—*Ribini*, alias Lance Corporal Raisumai, former member of the Bodo Security Force (BdSF)

LIKE THE WOMEN MILITANTS IN NAGALAND, THE WOMEN cadre of the United Liberation Front of Asom (ULFA), which bred militancy in Assam for decades, are high on ideology and commitment to their outfit.

Recruitment to ULFA, formed in 1979 to attain a sovereign socialist Assam by an armed struggle, was in full swing in 1987 when Pranati was contacted by an ULFA activist. ULFA was in need of a large number of youth it could send for arms training. Its leaders had linked up with Nagaland's rebel outfit, the NSCN, as well as Burma's (Myanmar) Kachin Independent Army (KIA), to train their cadres. ULFA had already sent its first lot for training to Myanmar camps in northern Burma to be trained by KIA which was experienced in jungle warfare as it was then fighting the Burmese junta.

Pranati

In 1986, ULFA had started to set up its own camp in the Tinsukia and Dibrugarh areas of Assam. It had just launched its controversial fund-raising campaign which, it was alleged, was actually extortion. When Pranati, a school teacher in Nalbari village on the Assam–Bhutan border, was reached out to by ULFA, it was well on its way to becoming one of the most violent and dreaded rebel groups in the northeast region of India, which had for decades been spawning bloody separatist movements. By 1987, ULFA was running a parallel government in Assam.[20]

20. Rajeev Bhattacharya, *Rendezvous with Rebels*, p. 168.

Pranati was just the type ULFA was keen to draft. The main considerations for recruitment are physical fitness, mental make-up, dedication to the cause and family background.[21] Not that the diminutive, frail girl would make a good fighter or have the physical strength to lug the arms and ammunition ULFA planned to surreptitiously procure from bordering countries. ULFA's military wing would not be the best place for her but she would be a perfect fit for the political wing ULFA was setting up to undertake indoctrination, teaching ULFA's history and philosophy in training camps and preparing publicity material. She was a no-nonsense, serious and studious girl. The ULFA recruiter was spot-on in his assessment of Pranati though he did not know that in a matter of years she would become the ULFA cultural secretary and the only woman in its apex body consisting of ULFA founders Arabinda Rajkhowa, Chairman, Anup Chetia, General Secretary, Paresh Baruah, Commander-in-Chief and Chitraban Hazarika, Secretary of Finance.

Pranati met all the ULFA requirements for recruitment. She was above eighteen years of age, highly educated with a post-graduation degree in the Assamese language, and single. Above all, like most of the youth of Assam, she was as disillusioned with the peaceful and democratic efforts of other organizations like the All Assam Students Union (AASU) and Assam Jatiyatibadi Yuba Chatra Parishad (AJYCP), the Assam Gana Sangram Parishad and even the Asom Gana Parishad (AGP), the political party which swept to power in 1985 to drive out illegal immigrants from Bangladesh into Assam and a separate homeland.

The young teacher became an ULFA over-ground worker. For two years Pranati held village meetings for ULFA propaganda,

21. Author's interview with Anup Chetia, Guwahati, 8 January 2016.

motivated people to join the ULFA ranks and provided shelter to ULFA men. During this time she was under observation of ULFA leaders. Working at the grassroot level was a test to determine if she was mentally and physically fit to be sent to a training camp. At the training camp the new recruits were screened to assess whether they should be assigned military work or sent to the political wing.[22] In 1990 she joined the ULFA political wing as a full-time cadre member. In the very same year ULFA was proscribed by the Government of India as a terrorist group.

In August 1990, Pranati was sent to ULFA's Sibsagar district camp. She became a student of the first batch to be given political training by ULFA. Of the forty youth in the batch there were about a dozen girls. Though she was not to be part of the military wing, she had to undergo a month-long basic training which was the same for men and women from either wing. The prescribed schedule was physical exercise and daily drill, arms training, ambush training, learning intelligence gathering, the art of communication, preparing a safe house, collecting information and passing it on further or to the intended person, and lessons in ULFA ideology.[23]

After her training she returned to Nalbari and in November 1990 was sent to the Lakhipathar headquarters of the ULFA commander-in-chief on the border of Dibrugarh and Tinsukia districts. Here Pranati was amongst the five girls invited to participate in the General Council meeting to be held in the adjoining Saraipung training centre and share their experiences as motivators. But before the meeting could take place the camp was attacked by security forces. She saw action for the first time.

---

22. Author's interview with Anup Chetia, Guwahati, 8 January 2016.

23. Author's interview with Anup Chetia, Guwahati, 8 January 2016.

Though Pranati was rather new to camp life, having been there just four or five days, she knew what a whistle sound meant at midnight. She was asleep when the whistle blew. She realized they had been attacked by security forces. The first line of defence made up of armed men and women was posted about one kilometre from the main camp. The sound of firing was all around and she realized that her comrades were in combat with security forces to allow those at the camp to escape. Following instructions given during training she ran to the field in the camp along with the others. The order given was for the thirty-odd women members present to break into pre-assigned groups and make their escape. The leaders of the groups had been decided in advance.

Pranati followed her leader on a five-hour trek through the forest to a village on its fringe and to a safe house there. Here the group was split further into five-member groupings. Pranati was in pain. She had hurt her foot and it was decided that she would find it difficult to walk on. But they had to move on. After receiving first aid, Pranati was asked to ride pillion on the cycle of one of the boys. The bicycle ride lasted five hours, after which her group reached a village in another district.

Here Pranati was asked to hide. She moved in with a family and for cover pretended to be a visiting relative. She had been instructed to live with the family and wait for communication from her leader. As she nursed the sore on her foot, Pranati had to do household chores like other members of the family. After a week she received orders through the communication network spread over villages to move on and join her organization. In 1991, Pranati was arrested for the first time. She had finished addressing a motivational meeting in Lakhimpur district and was moving to a 'sympathizer's' house in the village to stay the night when the CRPF (paramilitary force) arrived for a search operation. She could not manage to escape and was arrested. She was released after three months and there was no conviction. She returned to her organization to continue life underground. Two years later, in 1993, Pranati did manage to escape being caught by security forces in another encounter.

At that time she was in an ULFA district camp in Bhutan. ULFA had in 1990 set up camps in the forests of southern Bhutan. Here, as many as 2,000 cadres were estimated to be in ULFA general headquarters, council headquarters, security-cum-training camp and the Enigma Force (ULFA's exclusive strike group) base camp here.[24] Pranati had gone for her bath to a nearby waterfall outside the camp when a mortar fell right next to her. She understood the camp was under attack by security forces. She ran to the camp periphery and called out to one of the boys to hand over her clothes and survival kit which every member of the cadre had to keep handy. The kit contained a knife, needle, a kilo of rice, a matchbox and a sheet of polythene to help them survive when hiding in a forest.

She joined a group of twenty of her comrades and made her way into the surrounding jungle. They walked in the forest for three days, stopping to cook at night when the fog would give cover to the makeshift kitchen fire. Not only had they been instructed how to survive in the dense forest but also how to behave when they came across elephant herds or bears sitting in trees overhead. The simple rule was not to run or disturb them. They had been instructed to follow the rule 'Live and let live'. It was not the animals that they had to fear. It was the security forces that presented the gravest danger. They had to ensure they were not spotted by them. The group established a

24. South Asia Terrorism Portal, Institute for Conflict Management.

temporary camp when they found the right spot in the forest. The ideal place for a camp, they had been taught, was near a water source like a river or waterfall and not too far away from a village from where they could procure food. The villagers also helped in establishing contact with their organization boys of the village. They waited at the temporary camp till they were given the all clear to return to the main camp.

It was a tough life for Pranati but she took it in her stride. 'Mosquito-filled nights, danger of wild animals, simple meals, no bathroom and minimal amenities in a jungle camp cease to be discomforts when the mind is tough,' she says when I ask how she coped with it all. She does confess it was a life she had not really expected. 'When I decided to join the movement, I did not even ask what going to a training camp would mean in terms of physical comfort. How can you when one is dedicating oneself to a struggle?' Her life with ULFA has been all about dedication, discipline and following the orders of her senior leaders.

It was in April 1996 while at the ULFA district camp in Bhutan that Pranati was given a command she had never received in all her six years as an ULFA operative. Though she was known to be a disciplined soldier and the cultural secretary of the Central Executive Council, she decided do something she had never done before. Pranati resisted carrying out her senior's order. Paresh Baruah, founding leader of ULFA and commander-in-chief of its military wing, directed her to get married in the next two days. Pranati argued with her commander. She did not want to get married. 'I told him I wanted to dedicate my life to the organization.' Her senior brushed her objections aside and told her to leave the thinking to him. That was the end of the conversation. A word from the leader was nothing short of a command for her. Pranati walked back to the living quarters she shared with other girls to tell them what the commander had just ordered. While she showed little excitement, her friends were all agog. Getting married to whom? they asked. To their surprise and even amusement, she said she did not know.

She turned right back and returned to her chief to ask the name of her husband-to-be. 'I had not even thought of it when I was handed out the order.' Why? I ask her, bewildered at her lack of interest in the man she was to be married to. Like a disciplined soldier she replies, 'The directive itself was far more important for me than the name of the man Paresh had decided I was to wed. I had unquestioning faith in my commander. Whatever he decided would be in my best interest.'

In the afternoon of 21 April 1996, Pranati Deka took an oath with ULFA Finance Secretary Chitraban Hazarika to face all difficulties and adversities together. The oath paper was signed by them with Commander Baruah and other camp mates as witnesses. In accordance with the ULFA Bibah Upvidhi (marriage manual) the two were now married. A simple celebratory feast of rice, dal and meat curry followed. Later the evening was filled with song and dance. Folk dance and song were an integral part of camp evenings because of the organization's emphasis on the traditional culture of Assam. Pranati herself was a trained violin player. The wedding evening was the perfect occasion for her to give a performance. To her regret she was unable to do so. Her violin, which she had brought with her to the ULFA insurgent's camp, had fallen casuality to the humidity in the forest.

While Pranati was sad that she had been commanded to get married, she was happy at the choice of husband by her leader. She was confident that there could be nothing wrong with him as a person because 'he also belonged to the cadre'. She had worked with him and 'knew him' since 1989. But it was a working relationship and that too not a close one, Pranati points out. Chitraban, who had been arrested in 1992, had joined the camp after his release from jail a month before the wedding. Pranati and Chitraban were given family quarters in the camp for three months after their marriage. Once again came an order from the leader which, like it or not, had to be followed. It was decided that Chitraban go into hiding in a camp in Bangladesh. Pranati had to stay back in the Bhutan camp. For the organization it was of little consequence that the newly married couple would not be able to live together. Husband and wife were able to meet a year later, only for a couple of minutes. By then Pranati was in the last few days of her pregnancy and on her way to a Thimpu medical centre (Bhutan was considered a safe place for ULFA cadres) for her delivery. Chitraban was returning to the Bhutan camp from Bangladesh and the two met briefly somewhere on the way.

Pranati had to leave the Thimpu hospital as her blood group AB was not available there. The doctors saw her delivery as a high-risk one and she was advised to go to Delhi. She had little choice but to take a risk and travel undetected to Delhi. Here too her blood group was unavailable and she had to rush to Mumbai. Her baby was born in Mumbai at the Jaslok Hospital. It is alleged that a big corporate house with tea gardens in Assam paid her hospital bill. Is it true that her medical bills were picked up by the Tata Tea Company? I ask. 'Yes,' she says. 'It was financial support and not extortion,' she emphasizes in a firm voice. Her son was only seven days old when Pranati was arrested in August 1997. The black and white picture of her handing over the infant wrapped in a shawl to a policewoman on her arrest shows the emotion on her face...something rare for Pranati. When she was arrested, she was one of the senior ULFA leaders on the wanted list of the police. The police were on her track and picked her up at the Mumbai airport. She spent nine months in jail. After her release on bail she returned to the Bhutan camp in July 1998 along with her infant son. Her husband was in a camp in Bangladesh.

While her little son attended school at the Bhutan camp on her return, Pranati continued to carry on her task for the next five years as a motivator, moving from village to village, holding meetings and seminars. It was not a normal married life nor was the bringing up of her child normal. How did Pranati cope with a married life filled with separation and bringing up a child while being underground? 'It means little when there is a cause to fight for.' She hesitates then adds, 'Yes, I do feel my son's education did suffer because of my absence.'

In October 2003 Pranati was arrested again. 'I was on my way back to the camp after addressing a meeting at Goalpara. To return to the Bhutan camp from Goalpara I was required to enter the adjoining Meghalaya state. I had been warned by the boys accompanying me that the situation was tricky as the police were on the lookout for me.' The fallback plan was to head for Bangladesh where her husband was in hiding if she felt that returning to camp could lead to her getting caught. Pranati was apprehended in the border village of Phulbari in the Garo Hill district of Meghalaya. According to media reports, Pranati was travelling in a bus with her son when she was apprehended. She was planning to cross over to Bangladesh to join her husband after getting treatment for her child who was suffering from malaria.[25] This was the beginning of a seven-year prison stint for her. TADA (Terrorist and Disruptive Activities [Prevention] Act, in force from 1985 and repealed in 2004) was slapped on her. Pranati's husband too was arrested in November 2009. Her son moved in with his grandparents to continue his education.

25. *The Telegraph*, 26 October 2003.

Pranati was released on bail in 2010 as was her husband. She returned to her husband's family in Nagaon about 120 kilometres east of Guwahati. As she came out of hiding to live with her husband in Guwahati, Pranati saw her life take another turn. Just about a year later (February 2011), ULFA leaders announced that its General Council had decided that they sit for talks with the Central Government without any precondition. The decision to talk to the Indian government was rejected by Paresh Baruah. ULFA cracked and two groups were formed: ULFA Anti Talks Faction (ATF) and Pro Talks Faction (PTF). Pranati went along with Arabinda Rajkhowa and in October 2011 was appointed by him as a member of the steering committee set up to go into the details of the peace process. In August 2012, the ULFA split became formal when Paresh expelled Rajkhowa. He renamed the ATF as ULFA (Independent) and went into hiding on the Myanmar border and set up camp.[26]

*

Years of hardship in jungles, a disrupted married life and a difficult childhood for her only child to fight the Indian State and now to sit and talk peace with it. Has it been worth it? Does she regret this? I ask. 'One has to and should give up things for the larger interest and gain,' is her reply. Where is the gain? You have not achieved what you sacrificed your life for? I persist. Pranati refuses to be provoked or give up on her stand. She settles back into her chair, pushes back the bangles on her wrist, puts down her teacup as if readying for a speech. 'There is nothing wrong in going to the talk table. It is just another route to achieve what we set out to do. We have just

26. South Asia Terrorism Portal.

changed course, not the goal. The cause remains unchanged. I agree that we may not achieve fully what we set out for in the beginning. But this is what negotiation is all about. Also ideas evolve. There is nothing wrong in this process.'

Pranati's life is all about being dedicated to the cause of an Assam of her dreams. She is not disappointed that ULFA may not get 100 per cent of what she has sacrificed so much for. 'It is not only me. So many young boys and girls died in the ULFA Students' Movement. No sacrifice or life or effort is a waste. It is a contribution to a process. In a journey so many things happen before you reach your destination. Someone has to do things for the coming generation and the future. It does not matter if they are not going to reap the benefit.'

This leads me to ask why she has then chosen a path different from her leader Paresh Baruah on whose mere command she gave up her resolve to never marry. 'At some stage each one has to take a decision according to one's thinking. He has taken his decision. I have taken mine.' It is easy to visualize her at a covert village meeting addressing young men and women and convincing them of the ULFA ideology. The words of Pranati the Motivator bear her conviction with ease. No wonder they proved to be the fatal weapon against the establishment and security forces. ULFA leaders like her do not need a gun for their fight. They use their speech instead.

Is it tougher for women in the camps than it is for men? I ask. No, says Pranati. 'In our organization, gender is not an issue. Men and women are treated equally in dealings with each other, receiving training including in arms, facilities extended as well as being allotted tasks. However, it is the men who spot talent and recruit boys and girls. First they work over-ground and their dedication and aptitude is evaluated. Then they are sent to camps. Once they come to camp and are trained, their skills are assessed by the commander. He decides which wing of the organization the person is best suited for. Some are sent to the army camp and field work and others are inducted into the political stream.'

Describing the task of the likes of her in the political wing, Pranati talks of what their training comprises. 'We are educated in the aims and objectives of ULFA, the topics to speak on during village meetings and seminars, how to live and mingle with families when in villages and how to behave in public.' Everyone is given a basic training in use of arms, how to act during a confrontation with security forces while in the camp or outside, escape plan, survival in the forest if alone, reassembly and how to think on their feet if they are in a village hideout and confronted with security forces. 'We are told to be prepared for all eventualities at all times.'

While evaluation of skills has little to do with gender, Pranati's experience shows that 'women are good intelligence gatherers. Men get identified very fast by the police. Women can disguise themselves and they are also good actors. It is easy for women to melt into a family when in a village or town and throw search parties off track.' According to her assessment, women cadres have made not only a notable contribution to ULFA but also great sacrifices. 'They are mentally strong and have not flinched in the face of adversity. They are disciplined, dedicated and motivated. They have displayed full confidence and unquestioned loyalty to their leaders.'

When I broach a subject I am convinced she will find difficult to justify and defend the top leadership that ordered the action, Pranati remains unruffled. I am not surprised. Remaining calm in the face of challenges is her nature. 'I have been trained to convince people and not get angry. I can do this because I believe in what I tell them.' I ask her about the alleged extortion by ULFA cadres as a source of money for their cause, and to shore up finances. 'You call it by that word. We call it financial support.' She amplifies her point by denying large-scale extortion. 'There may have been stray incidents of extortion but they were not ULFA boys. We just got a bad name.' For Pranati it is the goal that is of paramount importance not the means used by ULFA leaders to achieve it. She justifies them all.

The only time I see a flash of anger on her face is when I show surprise at a highly educated person like her choosing to opt for a dangerous life with a banned outfit. But the glimpse of anger passes quickly. Pranati keeps her voice soft and sweet, deftly hiding the steel in her response. 'I am confused by what you are saying. Are you trying to tell me that it is bad for the educated to fight for their country?' She has me cornered. Pranati is ready for a debate on country, cause and the justification of going to any extent to fight for what one believes in. I back off, startled at the aggression she can pack into that slight form of hers. Is it her gentle persuasive manner of speaking that is misleading or is that her asset?

1991 was a testing year for ULFA. Since the November of 1990 the rebel group was being hounded and challenged by the Indian Army intent on wiping out insurgency from Assam. In November 1990, after the state was put under President's Rule, the army had launched Operation Bajrang, one of its biggest crackdowns followed by Operation Rhino in September 1991 to flush out ULFA cadres from their camps. ULFA had been declared a terrorist organization (1990) and banned by the Central Government under the Unlawful Activities (Prevention) Act of 1967. ULFA camps had been destroyed by the army. Hundreds of ULFA guerrillas had been apprehended and soldiers had virtually sealed routes used by them to slip into neighbouring states. Though the army was hot on their heels,

ULFA was far from broken. In fact, it increased violence by killing political leaders from the Congress party, eliminating informers and attacking army convoys.

Santana

It is the women cadre that kept ULFA 'alive' during the days of Operation Bajrang and Operation Rhino, says Santana Phukan Baruah who enlisted for the ULFA in 1990 when she was a student, and worked for the underground outfit for almost two decades. 'We used to give cover to men when they had to move from one hideout to another. We hid pistols in the clothes we were wearing and transported them for the boys. We kept up the communication network between camps and leaders by carrying letters and even passing oral messages about discussions, plans and development of the outfit from one leader to another. We took active part in organization work.' Acting as a courier of letters demands utmost secrecy and the women showed they were good at it. 'The letters, including the address on the envelope, are in code. Even the courier does not know the letter's final destination. She only knows who has handed it to her and who she has to give it to. This she has to keep secret and not disclose to even another cadre person.'

Her daring exploits show why guerrilla leaders farm out certain underground assignments exclusively to women. Women are considered the best to gather information, furtively ferry arms and ammunition, act as couriers of missives and operate safe houses.[27]

It was sometime in 1991, when Santana was travelling from

27. Author's interview with ULFA leader Anup Chetia, Guwahati, 8 January 2016.

Morigaon district to Nagaon district in Assam, that her bus was stopped at the Bebezi police checkpost. Her heart skipped a beat. Hidden in her blouse was a letter for Anup Chetia, the ULFA general secretary. The army men asked everyone to disembark for a search. Santana, known in the outfit as Rimu Mohan, defiantly remained sitting in the bus. Before Santana was ordered at gunpoint to get out, she had made a slit in the seat cover and pushed in the letter, hoping that it would not be discovered.

That was not all that Santana had to hide. Camouflaged by vegetables in a basket at her feet was a pistol she had to transport. It was time for Santana to put up an act. She started to behave as a student in a hurry to get to her college. Grumbling about the search, she asked the security men to hurry so that she would not be late. Displaying her books and her student identity card for all to see, she taunted the search party to even look into the basket of vegetables. Because of you all we can't even study, she berated them, while her heart pounded so loudly that she feared it could be heard by the others. Her audacious behaviour saw her through. The pile of vegetables lay undisturbed, hiding the pistol beneath. The tear in the seat too went unnoticed.

There were several instances during 1991 when Santana had to use her wits and her acting skills. Raids and searches had put the men virtually out of action. The chances of getting nabbed were at an all-time high. Yet communication amongst senior leaders scattered in various hideouts was imperative. It was left to the women cadre to be couriers of messages and arms besides arranging hideouts for the men during this time.

It was in the April of 1991 that Santana had to hide and nurse two of her injured comrades. They had moved in with a family of ULFA sympathizers in Dimuguri village in Nagoan district. The men were being administered a saline drip when the army, acting on information about hiding militants, encircled the village. Santana decided to act as an idle woman of the family sitting outside her home to pass the time. She saw an army vehicle driver approach her along with a soldier holding a map. The soldier asked if the pond she was sitting beside was the one marked on the map. The driver said that it did not appear to be the right one and then he gave her a conspiratorial wink. Santana nodded in agreement and sent them off in the opposite direction.

Santana was not the least surprised by the driver helping her out. ULFA operatives were often aided by sympathetic villagers and even policemen. This was one of the main reasons, besides unfamiliarity with the local language and topography, that made it difficult for the army personnel to achieve greater success in Operation Bajrang and Operation Rhino.[28] The likes of Santana took full advantage of this.

While she was undergoing training by ULFA seniors, she had been told the pattern an army search party follows. As one batch leaves, another follows a little later for fresh interrogation and search. She knew another batch would come in the next half hour. She rushed indoors and, using her medical training, removed the needle for the drip from the arms of the men. Then she quickly gathered the village people and asked them to help the injured escape via unmarked paths. She instructed the young boys to move out three cars, some motorcycles and six bicycles that were parked there for the use of the insurgents so she would not be asked why the family had so many vehicles.

Santana then collected the children of the family around the dining table and sat down with their books as if she was helping

---

28. *India Today*, 31 March 1991, story by Farzand Ahmed.

with their studies. She wrote out little chits for the children informing them what to say if questioned by the security forces. She also instructed the adults to pay close attention to what she would tell the army men so that they could repeat the same story when quizzed. The most important task still remained. She had with her important letters and documents meant for the ULFA leaders and they had to be hidden. Santana decided that the best place to conceal them would be in the underpants of the children!

As anticipated, the soldiers returned and asked who she was. Santana told them she was a daughter of the family and was helping the children with their school work. They searched the house looking for the ULFA insurgents and any incriminating evidence. The adults repeated Santana's lies and the children as instructed started to wail when the house was turned upside down and the adults interrogated. The men decided to leave when they could find nothing. Santana had even been able to explain the medicines left behind by her comrades by rattling off which family member was taking which capsule for which ailment. As soon as the army left, Santana escaped and, helped by the sympathizers in the village, joined her comrades. She told the family she had been hiding with that if the security men returned to look for her, they should tell them that she had gone back to her college in Guwahati to take her exams.

'I am a good actor and that saved me many times,' Santana says with a smile. The very next morning Santana made another cheeky escape. Required by her seniors to attend the ULFA Raising Day celebration on 7 April 1991 in Shillong in Meghalaya, she decided to use public transport to go to Guwahati. Hidden in her bag was a pistol and an angocha (traditional scarf) to present to her leader at the event. She flagged down a bus. As she got in, she realized that all the passengers in the bus were uniformed security personnel. Santana knew that she would arouse suspicion if she hurried out of the bus. She decided to travel with them, casually placing the bag near her seat. Luckily for her the bus was going only up to Sonitpur, a destination just twenty minutes away. When she learnt this she started to chide the driver for not telling her that the bus was not Guwahati-bound. The men in the bus tried to pacify her. Fearing that this would lead to a conversation in which she may be asked uncomfortable questions, Santana started to complain of motion sickness caused by the drive. She declined the water offered to her and placed her head on the headrest of the seat in front of her. Then she shut her eyes and waited desperately for the moment she could hop off the bus. When the bus reached its scheduled destination she complained to the driver even more for effect. Santana took another bus and travelled undetected to Guwahati and further on to Shillong.

It is with some pride that Santana declares that she has never been arrested or killed anyone. 'I was trained by experts like Meghali Kharguria and Moni Hazarika. The girls in ULFA are daring and motivated. They are in the military wing too. They are also given sentry duty in the camps like the boys. Most of the leaders have women guards. Many have died fighting security forces to enable leaders to escape. I remember one of the girls from the military wing, Mommy, was killed in a confrontation with security forces while on guard duty. These women joined before me. Among the first batch of women cadre was Shanti Rajkumari alias Tara Bujar Baruah. Boys and girls are treated the same in the organization. Everyone cooks, washes clothes or does whatever chores are required in the camp. Like the boys, the women are sent either to the operational wing or the political wing according to their capabilities.'

Besides protection duty (guarding leaders), ULFA women have taken part in combat operations like the 2006 Moran encounter with the police. Two to three women were in the Moran encounter but managed to escape.[29] Two years later, ULFA's Teji Mala Rabha was arrested and wounded when there was an encounter with the police and army at Gambil Apel. In August of 2008, the self-styled lance corporal of ULFA's military wing was arrested while she was moving with explosives. Mamoni alias Kusum Dihingia, a second lieutenant in ULFA, was arrested with her eight-year-old child in the bomb blast in Guwahati's Fancy Bazar.[30] ULFA's 28th Battalion, the most lethal and dreaded of its battalions, had women fighters. Almost two per cent of the battalion's strength was made up of women who were trained killers.[31] In 1999, during the Khanapara (Guwahati) encounter, the police were baffled when they saw an ULFA operative firing with one hand while looking ahead instead of at the men behind. In the fading evening light, it seemed the person was protectively carrying a bundle in the other hand. The police thought it unusual that the person was firing without looking back and running to make a quick getaway, and was not letting go the bundle to make escape easier. Since the person was heading towards a dead-end, the policemen were ordered by their senior not to shoot to kill. When they caught up with the armed insurgent they discovered it was a woman and the bundle she was carrying was her infant child. Interestingly, the child was taken by the police and brought up

---

29. Author's interview with a police officer.

30. Sanghamitra Choudhury, *Women and Conflict in India*, p. 109, Routledge/Taylor & Francis, India, 2016.

31. Author's interview with a police officer who served in Guwahati, January 2016.

in an establishment for children of terrorists run by the police. The mother surrendered.[32] On 15 September 2009, Devika Gohain, second lieutenant of the 28th Battalion, was arrested by the army and almost a month later two women of the same battalion were arrested in the Hengrabari area of Guwahati.

The 28th Battalion, which had Paresh Baruah as its commander-in-chief and Mrinal Hazarika as its commander, was one of three battalions that in March 1996 went on to make up ULFA's military wing, the Sanjukta Mukti Fouj. Not only were women rank holders in the 28th Battalion but they were also part of ULFA's Enigma Force or Group, which excelled in hit-and-run operations.

'I know how to use a pistol and gun but I was never involved in any fighting as I was not in the Arms Group (militant wing). I was in the Political Group where we were taught to use our words as bullets,' says Santana. Effective use of words is the arsenal of a motivator. What to say and when to say it is taught during political classes. 'We were instructed in how to answer questions during interrogation if apprehended by security forces. We were told to give limited information. The strategy was to disclose just one or two facts so that less of the cadre would be harmed. How to talk oneself out of a difficult situation was an important part of the political training.'

The biggest contribution by ULFA women during the days when the men were in hiding was motivating people outside the organization to come to their help. 'We realized we needed the support of the people in the village to operate as sometimes we were all alone. We would tell them about our work and cause. When our men or leaders were rounded up by security

32. Author's interview with a serving police officer who had taken part in the encounter, Guwahati.

forces, the villagers would confront them and by sheer mob power bring them back. We turned the common folk into ULFA sympathizers and they would protect the leaders by not disclosing who they were. There have been instances when our boys and leaders were brought back from jeeps of the security forces.'

Santana had been with ULFA for just about a year when she made the great escape. There was always a high risk of getting caught by security forces while transporting arms or carrying letters. The consequences that would follow were well known. What were they instructed to do in such a situation? Shoot at the security forces, shoot themselves or swallow a suicide pill so that no vital operational information could be elicited from them? 'ULFA does not have this culture. It is very good of our leaders not to instruct or expect us to kill ourselves. Instead we are trained how to handle interrogation so that the least damage is done to us as individuals as well as the outfit.'

Her joining ULFA was not something she had planned for. She was a nineteen-year-old, studying for a BA degree in Guwahati, when she was informed that her maternal uncle, none other than Arabinda Rajkhowa, chairman of ULFA, had called for her. She was keen to visit him not for his political activities but for the fact that that she had not met him in years since he had gone underground. The message was conveyed to her by Subham Saikia, the head of the family she was staying with to pursue her studies as her parents lived in Nakhat village (PO Khaloighugura) Sibsagar district.

It was in 1990, during the puja holidays, that Santana, her cousin, the son of her maternal aunt, and another friend were taken by Subham to Rajkhowa's hideout in a village near Narainpur in Lakhimpur district by bus. After night fell they started to walk. Five hours later, Santana arrived at a house in a village which to her utter surprise was being guarded by armed girls. Amongst those on sentry duty was a sixteen-year-old girl called Mommy. She was ushered in to meet her uncle. He first enquired about the welfare of the family members. Then he asked Santana what she was planning to do after her graduation. She told him of her dream to study further and become a professor. The uncle told her that he would train her in the use of arms so that she could join the struggle for the sovereignty of Assam. Santana's only condition to joining up was that she be allowed to continue her studies also.

Santana was sent to a camp in the forest for a month. The camp housed thirty-seven boys and four girls, including Santana. Here she was taught how to use firearms. The training included attending political classes. Lectures by leaders informed them that ULFA's fight was one of Assam versus the Indian government and all those who opposed independence for Assam. They had to target the Indian Army and other security forces. The most important instructions were on how they were to motivate other young people to join ULFA.

On her return to Guwahati, Santana went back to college but was now part of the ULFA communication department, travelling often to village meetings in Tinsukhia, Goalpura, Kokrajhar, Dibrugarh and Shillong as a motivator. It was during this period that she also became a courier of secret coded messages as well as arms. Her knack for getting out of tricky situations as well as her ability to successfully carry important letters to and from senior leaders like Chairman Rajkhowa, General Secretary Anup Chetia, and Hirakjyoti Mahanta alias Naren Deka, Deputy Commander-in-Chief, was obviously taken note of. In 1993 Santana was sent to Kokrajhar district camp for further political training. Here she became the first woman to join ULFA's Kokrajhar District Council.

A year later, in 1994, Santana was ordered to go to an ULFA camp in Nagaland and join the ULFA 2nd Battalion. The camp had 300 inmates of which twenty were girls. It lay in a dense forest in the foothills of the Himalayas crisscrossed by rivers and waterfalls. Life at the camp was tough. The day began at 3.00 a.m. with drill. At 8.00 they had their first meal of the day. Then it was off to work collecting logs to make rope bridges across rivers and gathering firewood for the kitchen. Daily chores included pounding maize that was cultivated there for food, cooking and weaving shawls to wear. Sometimes they had to scour the hills for wild potatoes when they faced a food shortage at the camp. Since the camp was deep in the forest with no village nearby, they had to be self-sufficient. The only time they went to villages was to practise first aid and basic medicine that they had been taught in the camp class.

'We had to work so hard that we could fill a glass with perspiration every ten minutes,' she says with a laugh. Santana did more than all this. She also, along with some others, wrote the ULFA World Magazine, probably the forerunner of ULFA's mouthpiece called 'Freedom' or 'Swadhinata'. This handwritten propaganda magazine contained poems and articles explaining that ULFA had taken up arms not to kill but to protect themselves from the enemy (security forces of the State of India), how the culture and traditions of Assam were being eroded by 'Indians', how the locals should protect their heritage of weaving, farming, using brass utensils, folk song and dance. Four copies of the magazine were written out. Three copies were circulated amongst the camp inmates. One copy was sent out to a supporter in Guwhati who would photocopy it and distribute the copies.

When we talk about life at the camp there, I am taken aback by what she calls her fondest memory. 'I remember the time I was sent from there to Myanmar to participate in a cultural programme. I performed our Bihu folk dance there. I love dancing,' she says and her hands move to the husori (Bihu song) and the sound of the dhol (drum) only she can hear. 'I was the only woman sent by ULFA to participate in a joint celebration organized by the NSCN and ULFA.' Emphasis on Bihu is part of ULFA's commitment to preserve the traditions of their land. Paresh Baruah celebrates the Bihu festival in his camp on the India–Myanmar border, often dancing with the cadres.[33]

Our conversation often veers off from underground activity to music and Bihu and then the beautiful traditional sarong-like dress she likes to wear. Santana proudly tells me that most of her mekhela chadars are made of the local moonga silk. 'I prefer wearing our handloom. I learnt to weave at our camp in Nagaland. I don't weave now but buy only handloom,' she says with an engaging smile. 'Luckily for me, I didn't have to be in jungle uniform most of the time. Since I was working amongst the village people and had to merge with them, I got to wear our traditional dress. Of course it was not made of silk but cotton.'

After a six-month stay in the Nagaland camp, Santana returned to Assam and worked over-ground. In April 1996 Santana was sent to an ULFA camp again. This time it was a hideout in Bhutan. The camp was the venue for discussions on the restructuring of the organization. As many as 300 members had gathered of whom thirty to forty were women. They were to participate in crucial policy framing. It was at this meeting that ULFA leaders decided that four zones (east, west, south and central) be created to strengthen the top-down system

33. Rajeev Bhattacharya, *Rendezvous with Rebels*, p. 258.

of command and for better administration and operation. At the top of the chain was the central committee, followed by the zonal (mandal) committee and then the district (shakha) committee. By now Santana was considered a senior in the women cadre and was appointed the cultural secretary of the ULFA Eastern Council.

She returned to Dibrugarh, which was part of the eastern zone. Here she worked with the assistant in charge of the East Zone who was from ULFA's 1st Battalion. Six months later her senior leaders proposed that she marry him. In 1990, ULFA leaders had taken a decision to allow cadres to marry within the organization. 'They encouraged cadres to marry each other instead of someone from outside. I was also persuaded to do so. I resisted for a year, then I agreed as I found nothing wrong with the idea.' On 21 September 1996, Santana was married to Mrinal Hazarika who later on led A and C company of the 28th Battalion to announce a unilateral ceasefire on 24 June 2008. 'It was an arranged marriage. We knew each other but that is all,' she says, adding with a laugh, 'there were many eligible bachelors around but I preferred him because of his good personality, and I admired his work.'

Talking about her husband I ask if she, who was a non-combatant member of ULFA, knew that he was also the commander of the 28th battalion known for violence and extortion. 'Of course, but it was the need of the hour. Don't forget he is the same man who thought of peace.' Mrinal was arrested in 2005 and on his release on bail in June 2008 he was able to get two companies of ULFA's 28th battalion to get into the peace mode. Company B refused and went with the leader Paresh Baruah who revived the 28th battalion in his new camp on the India–Myanmar border.

Santana is happy with the peace process and content doing 'social work' with the Mahila Samiti (women's organization) of the colony where she lives in Guwahati. It is women grassroot ULFA workers that Santana is most concerned about during the peace process. 'Most of them are in a bad financial situation,' she informs. 'Those who have surrendered are paid Rs 3000 per month by the government. Those who have not come overground are waiting. Some of them are widows, others are living in designated camps. Those who are trained professionals can return to being teachers, nurses or doctors. But what will happen to those who are not much educated and have given so many years of their life to the organization? Where will they go? As part of the peace talks we are demanding a government job for such people. Please do write about this.' As the conversation takes on a sombre note, Santana wants me to make her a promise. 'I want you to definitely include something when you write.' Assuming it will be a plea to the authorities to do something for the women in need of financial aid, I give my word. 'Don't forget to write about my Bihu dance performance,' is what she says as a parting shot, taking me completely by surprise but showing me another side of her personality.

Ribini

While ULFA has the likes of Pranati and Santana, educated and from middle-class backgrounds, the Bodo separatist militant movement from Upper Assam mainly draws women for its cadre from the semi-literate, poor and underdeveloped districts of Bongaigaon, Kokrajhar, Darrang, Barpeta, Dhubri, Nalbari and Sonitpur. Ribini lived in Udalguri district, near Odla Khasibari village where in 1986, Ranjan Daimary founded the militant Bodo Security Force (BdSF) to fight for the sovereignty of Bodoland.

Ribini's dimpled smile is in full display when I go to see her at the hospital in the Mazbat Tea Plantation some 180 kms from Guwahati in Udalguri, Assam (now a district under the Bodoland Territorial Autonomous District governed by the Bodoland Autonomous Council). She has invited me to meet up with her at her workplace. Ribini is the ever-friendly nurse here, chatting gaily with the patients she is attending to. 'Why do you fall every day,' she asks a young man while dressing his wound. 'Can't see properly? I will test your eyesight next time you come here,' she says in mock admonishment. 'You don't need cough mixture. Your cough is not so bad. I think you are making an excuse so you can be home with your wife,' she tells another middle-aged plantation worker. She tilts his face and pours the syrup down his throat, teasingly refusing to hand over the bottle to him.

You are really enjoying your work, I comment when we step out for tea. I am surprised by her response. 'I am so bored with this work of dispensing medicines for coughs and colds and bandaging minor wounds. I miss the adventurous life I led when I was NDFB (National Democratic Front of Bodoland, a banned militant separatist organization) cadre,' she says in a conspiratorial undertone. This is not the first time Ribini has used her smile to mislead people.

Ribini or Raisumai, the name given to her when in 1989 she enlisted with the BdSF (later converted into the NDFB), has always been fully aware of what her smile can do. 'I always kept my cheek with the dimple towards the other passengers in the bus when I was transporting arms. I use my smile as a weapon,' she explains with a comradely slap on my back. This is exactly what she did when the man sitting next to her in a Dimapur bus started to slide his hand over her thigh. He would lean against her, suggestively brush against her side and grope her. Instead of protesting, she coquettishly smiled at him and flirtatiously held his hand. Unknown to the man, Ribini was actually preventing him from moving his probing hands further down and discovering the two pistols strapped to her thighs. Ribini had been ordered by her camp commander to deliver the arms to a BdSF rebel in another town. Ribini had learnt early that when on assignment she was on her own with only her wits to help her out. Danger did not deter Ribini. Instead it was exciting.

As Lance Corporal Raisumai she was hailed as the daring one in the outfit. Her ability to think on her feet and to bail herself out of trouble instead of relying only on what she had been taught during training at the camp was often appreciated. Not only did her seniors recognize her as a courageous person but also a meticulous planner and information gatherer. It was her diligent work and month-long reconnaissance that led to the 1994 UCO bank (United Commercial Bank) and LICI (Life Insurance Corporation of India) heist in the town of Dhekiajuli (Sonitpur District) Assam by BdSF and NSCN (IM) insurgents. Right after that, in November 1994, the BdSF was rechristened NDFB by Daimary following his rejection of the Bodo Accord signed by the All Bodo Students Union (ABSU) and Bodo People's Action Committee (BPAC) which had led the Bodo movement. Ranjan Daimary later confessed to the BdSF involvement in the bank robbery.[34]

Ribini's face lights up when she talks about it. 'It was a big job but I knew I would be able to pull it off.' For her daily trip to Dhekiajuli, Ribini discarded her camp uniform of blue tracksuit and army boots and dressed in the local dhokna. She hired a bicycle in town and pretended to be a woman out

34. *Assam Tribune*, 29 May 2010.

shopping for the family. At times she stood at the bus stop as if waiting for transport. But all the time she was watching and studying the bank. She carefully noted in her mind the number of employees, the time it was most busy with customers, the temperament of the guard at the entrance, his daily pattern, where the door and windows were located and, above all, the possible escape route.

Soon Ribini had drawn out a map which she modified and perfected over a month. Every evening at the planning meeting at the camp she presented a report to her commander. Her inputs were crucial for planning and executing the robbery. The morning after the robbery, when the spot was teeming with policemen, Ribini returned to Dhekiajuli to give back the hired cycle! This was her style...never to avoid security men but to come up close to them, sometimes smile and at times even suggestively brush them on the arm as she passed them by. The proximity she generated put her above suspicion. The security men either laughed at her or just ignored her unwelcome soliciting (as they mistakenly interpreted it to be).

'I used to play-act to get out of dangerous situations. Sab karna padta hai jaan bachaney ke liye.' (One has to do everything to save one's life). In 1993 her acting talent was put to test when she boarded a bus from a spot on the Assam–Arunachal Pradesh border where the BdSF had a camp. The public transport bus was rattling along from Rangapura to Rowta. An obviously pregnant young woman was sitting with her two male companions. Every now and then she would shift in her seat, holding her bulging stomach and obviously hoping the bus ride would end soon. The bus stopped for a lunch break. Barely had the passengers started to eat at the wayside eatery when they were surrounded by security personnel. Following a tip-off, they were searching for militants active in the area.

The woman's companions went pale. As the security men came towards them the pregnant woman had a bout of vomiting. She clutched her stomach and, reeling from nausea, put her head on the shoulder of her companion. The security men looked at her with sympathy and moved on. The woman looked exhausted and barely able to walk. She collapsed on the bench and pushed her untouched food away. Her companions signalled to the bus driver to carry on without them as the woman was in no condition to continue her journey. The bus and the security squad drove off. The woman and her companions suddenly got up and started to run towards the nearby railway station. The crowd stared at them in surprise. Soon there was laughter as onlookers called to the woman to take care of her shawl which had come undone and was trailing on the ground. Ribini ran even faster, holding the bulge on her stomach, and boarded the train that had just come into the station.

Like many times before Ribini had made another escape. The bulge on her stomach was made up of two pistols and ammunition strapped to her abdomen and camouflaged by the folds of her dress. Her task was to deliver the arms to a contact in Rowta. Ribini and the accompanying men were on an assignment from one of the BdSF camps deep in the jungle bordering Bhutan. By then the BdSF had established twelve camps in southern Bhutan on the border with India. These were destroyed in 2003 when the Royal Bhutan Army carried out 'Operation All', under pressure from India, to clear its territory of insurgents who had taken refuge there.

Even her family knew she could take on tasks others could not. Her two sisters and two brothers did little when after her father's death her mother's belly started to swell, leading the neighbours to make vulgar insinuations. Her father, though a well-to-do farmer, had died leaving no money. Sixteen-year-old

Ribini decided to take matters into her hands. She borrowed cash to take her mother to a doctor who diagnosed her with a large tumour in her stomach. Ribini had her operated upon. But after that Ribini did something that made her mother very sad and her siblings very angry.

She left home to join the BdSF men in the jungle camp. BdSF largely recruited from around Udalgiri in Darrang district of Assam. On 3 April 1989 at about 2.00 p.m. she told her mother that she was going to visit a friend. Instead, she boarded a bus for Ambagaon together with her sister's husband, Nagen Daimary. After a 20-km bus ride, she discarded her slippers for army boots provided by Daimary. Here they were joined by four other girls. Dressed in skirts and boots they started the trek towards the forest on the border with Bhutan. They walked all night, finding their way through dense vegetation and often scared of the wild animals they saw. Early next morning they reached a clearing in the forest which had five tarpaulin-covered hutments. This was the BdSF Sardamjhankea camp in Bhutan.

Ribini had barely a few hours to think of what she had done and what her action would lead to. In those few hours she felt scared of a life in the forest but soon she was in the presence of Premsing Brahma and Zubrang, known to her as terrorists and bomb-making experts with the BdSF. Ribini became a member of the fourth batch of the BdSF to be trained. Her trainers were Brahma (earlier chief of the Bodo Volunteer Force, the military wing in the Bodo movement, who surrendered with 200 cadre in 1993 after the Assam Legislature passed the Bodoland Autonomous Council Act and an interim Bodoland Executive Council was formed) and Zubrang, who was later killed in an ambush. It was a tough life, but Ribini took a liking to it when she realized that she was able to do things she had not thought she was capable of.

For twenty days, Ribini was required to be up at 2.00 a.m. when it was still dark. After a breakfast of noodles and a cup of Horlicks, she was made to learn marching for three hours, crawling, long and high jump, combat with and without arms and .303 rifle target practice. This was followed by classes and lectures on the outfit's mission. Then it was time for lunch, a hearty meal of meat or fish with noodles. After doing assigned chores like working in the kitchen or mess, it was time to retire for the day. Bedtime was 3.00 p.m. Camp discipline demanded that everyone retire early so they could be up by 2.00 a.m. the next day. Darkness came early to the camp area and it was important to ensure that there was no tell-tale light from the settlement.

For two years Ribini's assignment was to transport arms and ammunition to the camp, carry messages and to meet up with other leaders for planning operations. For this she had to travel far to Dimapur, Guwahati, Kokrajhar, Rangapura and even Kathmandu. Sometimes she had company but at times she had to walk through the forest all alone with just a 9 mm pistol for protection. The arms had to be hidden in the dress she wore to look like the local people. But she was never afraid and lucky never to be ambushed or take part in an encounter. She did, however, have to use her knowledge of first aid which she had acquired in Class 6 when she was part of the All Bodo Students Union volunteer force. When injured comrades were brought to the camp she attended to bullet wounds and fractures. From them she learnt about encounters with security forces and ambushes.

For another two years Ribini was sent to Bodo villages around Rangapura on the border with Arunachal Pradesh. Her assignment was to motivate young Bodo boys and girls to join the underground Bodo movement. She knew how to go about it as she herself had been recruited by Ranjan Daimary (who later formed the NDFB-RD faction), when she went to sing at a meeting addressed by him in her school. When he spoke of the fight for Bodo identity, for recognition of Bodo language and culture and a separate state for them, it resonated with her own thinking. Ribini held meetings and seminars in villages and was able to persuade a number of boys and two girls to join the camp for training.

After a one-year stay at the forest camp, Ribini made a visit to her home in Daifang (Kahibari) in Udalguri district. Her mother started to wail on seeing her, asking why she had saved her life if she wanted to leave them and run away to the jungle. Her siblings were also angry at her for going away. People from her village gathered to see her and she broke down. After a week, when Ribini decided to return to camp, her send off was with tears 'as if a married girl was returning to her husband's place.'

Ribini was now a wanted name for the security forces. News from home told her how her family was hounded by them for information about her whereabouts. As 1994 drew to a close, her brother-in-law was picked up, blindfolded and taken to an army camp. The security forces told her family to find her and ask her to surrender if they wanted to be left in peace. Her sister's house was often searched by security forces who told her to get Ribini to surrender or their lives would not be spared. Ribini was distressed that her innocent family members were being harassed on her account. She discussed the situation with her then commander-in-chief Bhupen Buhaithi (killed later in an encounter in Rowta). She told him that she could continue to work for him over-ground. He granted her permission and Ribini surrendered to the local police in 1995 with thirteen others in Pathorighat (Mangaldoi district). She felt a tinge of sadness when she had to part with her pistol which had been her constant companion in the jungle and on her assignments for six years.

*

Ribini talks with fondness not only of the pistol she had to give up but also her life as a rebel. Would she like to return to the camp? 'Nahin ja sakti, mazboori hai.' Laughing, she points to her 'mazboori'—her teenage son and six-year-old daughter around whom her life now revolves. She takes me to her small house in the campus of the tea estate and it is easy to see that she still handles all the difficult situations. She directs her husband to bring out tea and snacks. As he looks a wee bit lost, she tells him what to do. 'You can fry some bread for snacks and boil tea.' Then she settles down to talk while her son and husband keep up a steady supply of raw supari to which she is addicted. 'I am the sole breadwinner. I have to educate my children and keep the home fires burning with my salary of 5,000 rupees a month.'

Post surrender has been a tough life for Ribini, the NDFB daredevil. For her it has been far tougher than life in the forest camp in Bhutan or while on assignment. According to her, there was good food to be had at the camp and plenty of excitement. In fact, Ribini did not want to surrender. 'I had decided I would live in the forest camp and die there for the organization. I thought that I would not be accepted by my people on return. I thought no one will marry me as they had seen me looking pregnant (here she bursts into laughter). I decided to surrender only because of the pressure the security forces put on my people.'

After her surrender Ribini returned home for a few months. To her surprise she was shown respect by her people. 'No one asked any questions about my life in the jungle.' In exchange for surrender, Ribini was made many promises by the police. She was offered a job in paramilitary outfits but she declined. 'If I had taken up the job it would have meant giving information about the camps or even taking part in an encounter with my old comrades. I did not want to do this.' But Ribini realized she could not just sit at home. In December 1995, she left for Guwahati to work in a nursing home for some practical training. A job still eluded her. Finally, she had to fall back on her old contacts in NDFB. 'A senior from the NDFB (P) faction who had joined the peace talks with the government gave me a letter of recommendation and in February 2000, I got a job as a nurse in the tea garden hospital.' Was she given a job for fear of her organization? Once again Ribini breaks into her hallmark infectious laugh. Instead of giving a straight answer she says, 'I can't deny that we were a feared lot but the garden has a hospital and a hospital needs a nurse.'

Here she met Nagan Daimary, a contractor building roads in the tea plantation. Romance blossomed. The fact that Ribini had lived away from home in a forest camp was not an issue for Nagan. 'No one in our village or family and friends looks down on cadre.' A year later they married. Unfortunately, Nagan's contracts ceased after a while and since then the family has been under financial stress. 'I have no one to go to for help. Most of my comrades have surrendered, others have become old. In any case I am not in touch with the organization though I miss that life.' Ribini recalls that she decided to join the insurgents out of choice. 'I had realized that we Bodos had no ethnic identity outside our villages. When I went on school trips to Guwahati and Delhi, people did not know about our language or our culture. They looked at our dance and dress in wonder. They only knew us as people from Assam. The NDFB's fight for sovereignty made sense to me.' If Ribini had not gone into the camp for training, she would have tried her hand at being a professional singer. 'I was singing a Bodo folk song "shiv shiv baar barding"...(my heart is blowing like the wind...) at a meeting when I met Ranjan Daimary. My dream was to be a singer but I was so motivated by his talk that I decided to join his organization,' she recalls.

Does she feel that her days working for the NDFB and risking her life have been worth it since the NDFB has been talking peace with the government since 2005? Has she contributed to the NDFB achieving its objective? 'We have got only half of what we had dreamt about. This makes me sad. If some young girls were to ask me, I would tell them to go ahead and fight to get full autonomy. If I had to live my life again, I would follow the same course...probably not surrender because by doing so I have gained nothing. The government promised financial help but gave me nothing.'

Till the end of 2016 Ribini would call me to ask if I could help her find a more lucrative job in Assam. In her last call she said, 'Mein bahut pareshan hoon. Paise nahin hain. Mujhe surrender nahin karna chaihiye tha. Camp mein khush thi. Wish mein wahan hoti.' (I am very harassed. I have no money. I should have never surrendered. I was happy in the camp. I wish I was there). Now when I call her mobile phone, a recorded voice states that the number dialled is not reachable.

Manu

In the year 2012, persistent missed calls on any youngster's mobile phone in the villages of the Bodoland Territorial Area District (BTAD) in Assam meant only one thing. Outlaw Ingti Kathar Songbijit and his men were calling. It was the year

Songbijit, commander of the NDFB's Bodo army, had split with his leader Ranjan Daimary over the NDFB peace initiative with the Government of India. Vowing to carry on the NDFB armed struggle under his own leadership, his band of insurgents, now known as the NDFB (S) faction, were stepping up recruitment in the four districts (Kokrajhar, Baksa, Udalguri, Chirang) that constitute BTAD. Songbijit had already set up camp in the forests of eastern Nagaland (Myanmar) and wanted to build a trained cadre to take the movement forward.

During August 2012, 21-year-old Manu of Chirang district's Jwngmapuri village, received three missed calls on her mobile. She had been getting calls on her mobile from the unknown number since the last few days. Her father had died a few months back and her stepmother ill-treated her, demanding that Manu go and live elsewhere. Life had turned a living hell when her father had remarried. He started to treat her shabbily, always scolding her and insisting she do all the household chores. When her mobile registered a missed call from an unknown number for the third time in a span of days, a troubled and unhappy Manu decided to return the call.

The missed call was not only intriguing but in a way welcome for lonely Manu. The voice at the other end identified himself as Gundwi. Manu started a telephone friendship with him. Several conversations later he revealed that he was a member of the NDFB (S) and lived in the jungle. It made little difference to Manu. For her, he was someone to talk to and share her suffering. After three months of daily phone chats, Gundwi told Manu of the NDFB (S) women cadre who were trained in the forest. He asked her to join.

Manu agreed. 'I had nothing to lose. I did not know anything about the men in the jungle nor did I care,' she tells me during a conversation marked by long spells of silence and bouts of crying by her. In fact our first meeting is nothing short of a crying session for her. As I watch her, I find it hard to visualize her as a gun-toting member of the most dreaded insurgent outfit active in the northeast region today. When I meet her in Chirang district (Assam) in January 2016, she has already spent four and a half months in Goalpara District Jail and is out on bail. That explains why Manu's brother and stepmother (who according to Manu have no love for her) do not let her out of their sight even for a short while. They have stood surety for her bail and cannot afford to have her disappear. They fear the financial consequences they will have to face if she runs away or is taken away or even killed by NDFB (S) men fearful of her parting with information about them to the police and cannot be produced in court when required.

Manu alias W. Mwnfwi of the banned NDFB (S) outfit was arrested on 15 March 2015 by the Dhaligaon (Chirang district) police on charges of unlawful association, conspiracy and possession of firearms. According to the police records, Manu's disclosure led to the recovery of a grenade and arms from Subaijhar village (Chirang district) where she had hid for some time.[35] The police saw her as a prize catch as she was one of the twenty-two trained NDFB (S) women out of a cadre of 100 men on their wanted list.[36]

Her silent weeping turns into uncontrollable sobs when she relates how her stepmother treated her. It is easy to believe her when she says she saw Gundwi's offer as an opportunity to escape from a miserable life. In January 2013, she agreed to go to meet Gundwi in the village of Oxiguri, a two-hour drive from her

35. Case No. Dhaligaon 54/15 charged under IPC Section 121/121A/122/133 read with Section 4 ES Act, read with Section 10/13/16 UA (P) Act.

36. Author's interview with an Assam police official, Guwahati, 2016.

home. Gundwi sent a car to fetch her. During the drive Manu felt a little scared stepping into the unknown but 'I could not turn back'. The driver took her straight to Gundwi who she was seeing for the first time. There were two other boys with him. For two days Gundwi put them up in a separate house in the village. For the next three months, he moved them from village to village where they lived with families in their homes. He told them that soon they would be sent for training. The group was now joined by five other girls.

Gundwi hired a mini bus and sent Manu and the other girls to Guwahati in it. From there, as instructed by him, the group boarded a public transport bus for Dimapur in Nagaland. Here, as pre-arranged, they were met by a man. He had four young men with him. He took the girls and the boys by bus to a nearby village. Here he hired a ten-seater vehicle and took them to a village on the Nagaland–Myanmar border. After spending two days at the border village, Manu, along with the rest of the group, was directed to discard her traditional dress and change into a tracksuit and army boots. It was essential for the long and hard journey ahead.

For ten days Manu and her companions had to trek in a single file over mountains and through thick forests. They walked during the day and slept at night in villages en route. There was a change of guide after every few miles and they carried the rice for meals. They were men from the cadre and they kept informing the group about where they were heading. On the ninth day Manu's group was informed they had crossed into Myanmar.

On the tenth day they reached a cluster of small houses ringed by mountains through which ran a small river. Manu is not sure if Daka was the proper name of the village (in Myanmar settlements in which Buddhist villagers donate food to monks are called daka) but everyone at the camp referred to it by that name. This is where the NDFB (S) had its headquarters. The HQ consisted of five barracks with bamboo walls and roofs thatched with broad taal leaves. It housed about seventy boys. Manu and five companions were the 'first batch of girls to join the cadre here'. Nearby were camps of other banned outfits like the United Liberation Front of Assam, National Socialist Council of Nagaland and Manipur's People's Revolutionary Party of Kangleipak. The NDFB (S) camp comprised only Bodos.

For a month Manu's batch of boys and girls had to do hard labour during the day. They cut firewood, dug trenches, plastered the bamboo walls of the barracks with mud and repaired thatched roofs with new leaves. Evenings were devoted to a drill of physical exercises and training with fake arms. Manu was given the sophisticated M-16 gun for target practice only once during the entire two-month arms training. She missed the target by a wide margin! Manu's training ended in July 2013. By 2014, NDFB (S) reportedly had 270 men and women spread across camps in Nagaland and the Sagaing region of Myanmar.[37]

It was time to move out of the training camp and work for the organization while living with the local population in villages. Manu and two other girls and five boys were directed to go to Dimapur and from there take a train to Guwahati. From there they hired a car and drove to Bijni. Manu was given the mobile number of a contact in Bijni. After her call, the contact arrived and took them to Udalgiri village near Chirang. From there they were moved to the NDFB (S) unit which was camped in nearby Selekhaguri village. The commander of the unit was Dwisrang.

37. Author's interview with intelligence personnel in Guwahati, 2016.

Commander Dwisrang assigned Manu the job of cooking for the unit as well as to keep a look-out for approaching security forces. Manu's areas of operation were the surrounding seven to eight villages. She had to live in these villages from time to time with the locals and keep an eye on troop movement. Not only was she to monitor movement of security forces but also gather information about them from the villagers. She was provided a mobile phone to pass on information and intelligence to Dwisrang and a 9 mm pistol for self defence. At times she was tasked with hiding small arms and when at the unit camp, her job often was to guard arms and ammunition kept there. They boys were sent to distant places on assignment while the girls had to remain at the unit or nearby villages.

'I often asked Dwisrang why he was not sending me out though I was trained,' she says. The NDFB (S) by then was using women primarily for transfer of money, as couriers, movement of arms and to monitor and report movement of security forces.[38] Little did she know that she was actually performing a vital task for her organization by remaining undetected in villages and gathering information to know if security forces were approaching. Movement of forces was a crucial input for the NDFB (S) insurgents who were being flushed out by about 9,000 soldiers of the Indian Army and Central Reserve Police Force (CRPF) under 'Operation All Out.'[39] 'Operation All Out' was launched in February 2015 following the December 2014 massacre of non-Bodo tribes allegedly by NDFB (S) men in the BTAD districts of Sonitpur, Chirang and Kokrajhar.[40] More than seventy people were killed. In November 2014, the

38. Author's interview with an intelligence officer operating in Assam.

39. India Today news, 26 December 2014.

40. PTI, 25 December2014.

Assam police had already put Songbijit on its list of fifteen most wanted militants.

The prime task at that time for women cadres was to have information on movement of security forces well in advance so that the men could make a getaway. 'I did not know anything about all this,' Manu says to me.

It was clear that the insurgent leaders were feeling the heat of 'Operation All Out'. But they did not feel the need to tell the likes of Manu what was going on. In the first week of March 2015, Commander Dwisrang ordered Manu and others in the cadre to scatter and hide with friends and relatives elsewhere and wait to be contacted again. Manu could think of no other place than that of her sister's.

As anticipated, she did not receive a warm welcome when she reached there. Her sister, who runs a beauty parlour in Guwahati, was scared to keep her as she was aware that Manu had joined the NDFB (S) outfit and its members were being hunted by the police. Manu pleaded to be taken in for a few days as she had nowhere else to go. She could not return home because her stepmother had made it clear that she did not want her around. It was because of her that she had run away in the first place.

It was clear to Manu that her sister would not let her hide at her place for long. She became desperate to establish contact with her outfit so she could return to the camp. That was the only place she felt wanted. She was eager for news. Amongst the contacts provided to her in Guwahati by her leaders was that of the brother of one of her comrades in the outfit. If she could establish contact with her comrade she would be able to discuss what she should do next. She had been instructed by her camp commander not to use her mobile phone as it could be under police surveillance. To avoid a security breach she used her sister's mobile and at night made a call to her comrade's brother who was a driver in Guwahati.

The call turned out to be a fatal mistake. The police were tracking the phone of the driver as his brother was a known NDFB (S) operative. They heard Manu identify herself to him and ask where she could find her comrade. Unknown to Manu, the police were in hot pursuit of her. She was on their most wanted list of NDFB (S) women cadre. The police traced the owner of the number of the phone Manu had used to the owner of a beauty parlour near the Guwahati airport. The next morning they arrived at the saloon and picked up her sister.

Manu was blissfully unaware that her phone call the previous night had been tracked. She was asleep when the police led by her sister arrived to take her in. As she talks of her arrest, her tears start all over again. By now she has rolled her handkerchief into a small tight ball making no attempt to use it to wipe away her tears. She looks more angry than sad. She clutches her mobile even more tightly. Is she angry at herself for making that call that turned out to be a giveaway?

She looks away when I ask her why she is crying. Were you treated badly by the police? Did you have a rough time in jail? Do you regret joining a banned outfit? Do you want to go back to your comrades? My questions are met by silence. She continues to stare out of the door as if oblivious of my presence, back in her own troubled world. Nothing I say helps to pull her out of it. Not even admiration of the fluorescent nail varnish she is wearing elicits a response from her. I put my arms around her not only to comfort her but also to remind her of my presence. It doesn't help. We sit in silence. I wonder if this is a message for me to leave her alone. I offer her a tissue to wipe her tears. She responds with a faint smile and reaches out for it. She still does not speak as if she needs more time to decide whether she should talk to me or not. 'I used this nail colour because I am bored of the regular reds and pinks. Sometimes I do things out of the ordinary.' Talk of an understatement, I think but refrain from saying it for fear of pushing her back into silence. At least she has started to talk again.

When she starts to speak she keeps her voice low but steady. There is little hesitation when she answers questions. Does she know why she was arrested by the police? 'No,' says Manu. How can that be? Did she not know that she was part of an outfit declared a terrorist organization by the government? For the first time, Manu looks at me directly and with an unfaltering gaze, utters a firm 'No.' Her look challenges me to contradict her. I decide to let it pass and allow her to carry forward the conversation.

Manu tells me that the first time she became aware of the ideology and mission of the 'jungle men' was after joining them at the camp where she trained. In the evenings, she recounts, the leaders held seminars and talks for the new recruits. At these 'classes' they were told of the aim of creating a separate land for their people, free of other tribes and 'outsiders'. They all had to 'throw them out', fight the security forces for the creation of an independent Bodoland.

All this meant little to her. For Manu the camp was a place she had come to so that she could escape the drudgery at home and the temper of her stepmother. She could not bear the humiliation of being made to feel so unwanted by her. At the camp she had been welcomed and made to feel part of a family. She did not mind the hard work or the training. It was only at the Selekhaguri unit that she started to feel things were not going the way she had imagined they would. Manu felt under-utilized. Most of her time was spent in cooking for the unit or helping in the daily chores at the homes of those she was directed to hide with in villages. She tells me that once she even asked her commander why she had been trained in the use of arms if all she was to do was cook. He kept quiet, she tells me. It was then that she started to wonder if she had made a mistake joining the cadre.

Was cooking the only task assigned to her? I ask. Manu reveals that at times she was also asked to keep an eye on stored arms and ammunition when the men were away on assignment. She also discloses that once or twice she did transport small arms like pistols from one village to another. Since her area of operation was only seven to eight nearby villages, she had to walk short distances with the arms and hand them over at the other end as directed. Manu says she did not encounter any police or security men while she was ferrying arms nor ever have to use the 9 mm pistol given to her for her defence. She did use the mobile phone given to her to pass on ground information she collected by talking to locals about the presence of security forces and their movements.

Was the grenade she had hidden in Subaijhar and recovered by the police on the basis of information provided by her part of an assignment? Manu looks startled and in a stiff voice denies giving any such information to the police or recovery of a grenade. My question on her plans for the future is met with a deep sigh. Again she looks away from me and stares out of the door. She turns to me a minute later and asks me for some suggestions on how to move on. What about getting married and starting a new life? Is there a man in your life? I ask her. A smile plays on her lips only to be replaced by a wry look. She turns away again. Without glancing towards me she says almost to herself that she has no options but to stay with her stepmother who hates her. Manu gets some financial help from her sister but is not sure how long it will continue.

A long sigh from her signals the end of her conversation with me. I try to persuade her to step out for lunch. She declines. 'Don't you have a train to catch?' she asks. I tell her that I can postpone my return if she promises to spend more time with me. She nods her head and says, 'There is little left to tell. I wish I knew what to do next with myself. Even you don't have a suggestion, except marriage.' What's wrong with that? I counter. She smiles again as she waves a farewell. Then she laughs for the first time since we have met. It is so unexpected that I turn around. 'I will inform you when I find the right man,' she calls out after me.

I am still waiting for Manu to call.

Is it that Manu has yet to find her Mr Right or has she returned to a place from where telephone calls are forbidden? No return calls from Ribini and Manu always set me wondering. It is evident that for the likes of them return from a militant camp does not always have a happy ending.

MANIPUR

Dancing with Death

'It struck me then how women want to save lives and here I am, a woman, killing people without a thought.'

—*Purnima,* former member of the Kangleipak Communist Party (KCP)

WOMEN ULTRAS ARE COMMON IN MANIPUR. PREPAK (People's Revolutionary Party of Kangleipak), formed in October 1977, was the first to recruit women for its cadre. PREPAK's founder leader R.K. Tulachandra, kept women guards, right from day one. The women were recruited from the remote areas of Manipur where they found no employment despite being educated. PREPAK initially used them as auxillary medical staff, for movement of arms and couriers of missives. Manipur's PLA (People's Liberation Army formed in 1978) too had women in their cadre since the 1980s. Gun-toting PLA women in uniform were photographed while undergoing training. In early 1981, eleven girls from Manipur travelled with twenty-seven people to Kachin in upper Myanmar to set up a new camp after PLA's (Eastern Region) Choro camp was destroyed by the Home Guards in October 1980.[41]

Another batch of 100 PLA militants which set out for Saitang camp on their way to Kachin later in October 1982 included freshly recruited girls. They travelled for three months through thick wildlife-infested jungle to reach their destination.[42] Rough dangerous terrain and a taxing training schedule to match that for men were not the only challenges women had to face in their life as a guerrilla. While they interacted with their male comrades and lived in close proximity with them, the PLA women cadres had to adhere to a strict code of conduct.

41. Phanjoubam Tarapot, *Insurgency Movement in Northeastern India*, pp. 61, 120.

42. Phanjoubam Tarapot, *Insurgency Movement in Northeastern India*, p. 134.

In 1984, a Miss Lee alias Kamala Devi was beaten up by three of her comrades for having 'illicit relations' with leader Soibam Temba. The group of seventeen, of whom ten were women, were on their way to Kotlun village in the Eastern Naga hills. Temba decided to avenge the beating of his lady love. Some months later (January 1985) he ordered the shooting down of those who had thrashed Miss Lee. Five months later the romance between the two insurgents led to marriage at a camp of the Burmese rebel group, the Kachin Independence Army (KIA). Temba's act was seen as indiscipline and he was overthrown in a coup by his angry men.[43] This incident notwithstanding, PLA women were obviously taking part in combat by the 1990s. This was confirmed when two PLA women militants were shot dead in an army ambush in the Chandel district of Manipur in the late 1990s. They were on patrol duty.

Women are in the ranks of all of the several extremist groups operating in Manipur in the northeast, which touches the state of Nagaland to its north, Mizoram to the south, Assam to the west and Myanmar to its east. This state has earned the dubious distinction of today cradling the largest number of insurgent groups in India (a conservative estimate being seventeen). Most of them have split into several factions. Extortion is the main source of funding for most of them.

While Manipur has a large number of women ultras, they refuse to be written about. I did manage to meet a couple and they seemed happy to speak about their lives underground but were adamant that I would not write about them or identify them. The reason Leela (name changed), who for a couple of years was the personal bodyguard of the leader of her

43. Phanjoubam Tarapot, *Insurgency Movement in Northeastern India*, p. 135.

organization, gave for this reticence was that her leader would not like her to make the nature of her work as a militant public. Grace (name changed), who left her outfit three years ago after being a member of its 'fund collecting team', told me that her leader had denied her permission to give an interview. The same was the case with Meiranpi (name changed), who did patrol duty for two years and was in the ambush party. Why do they have to listen to their leaders now that they are no longer members of militant groups? I ask. They inform me that they are still watched by them and men from the 'gang' and cannot dare do anything against their wishes. Else they may be suspected of turning police informers. They are told that it is best to remain under the cover of anonymity for their own safety too.

It was in 1982 that Mercha (name changed) left the militant outfit she was with for twelve years. She is married to a person who was a senior leader in the organization and is now a teacher. Coming from a poor family, she was in need of money to care for her sick father and two younger sisters. She was first approached in 1978 by 'men who said they would pay me to write slogans on posters'. She had finished her matriculation and was unable to find any work. She had to go underground when the police swooped down on her village looking for insurgents. She was told by her unit leader to go with men from another group, the Mizoram National Front, to their camp in Bangladesh. In 1980 she married one of the men at the camp who was also from Manipur. In 1990, she returned with her husband and three children to Manipur and surrendered so she could 'bring up my children in my own country without fear of getting caught'. She wants to remain unidentified because she is afraid that her past, if known, may jeopardize her son's career with a government defence establishment. Do your children not know that you have been a militant? I ask. 'They may know, but I haven't asked them and they have never mentioned it,' is her answer.

Purnima

Unlike Leela, Grace and Mercha, Purnima knows no fear. She never has.

The feel of an icy hand in a cemetery in the dead of night would make most people jump out of their skins. Not twenty-year-old Purnima. Instead she leapt to her feet, her flick knife open and ready to boldly take on any threat. Through the darkness the whisper cajoled: 'Come with me.' She recognized the voice immediately. He had made this offer to her many times before when she was living with her brother in Imphal's west district. Why had this man followed her to the cemetery where she had taken refuge for the night after walking out of her stepbrother's house? Was he trying to take advantage of her now that she was alone with no place to go to? It will not be the first time for me, she thought. This was a familiar script in the life of Purnima, born to a mother gone insane and an unknown father.

If her life has been like a kaleidoscope where the slightest twist changes the entire pattern, the night in the cemetery was one such turn. Homeless Purnima was recruited by the rebel group Kangleipak Communist Party (KCP), an offshoot of PREPAK, floated in April 1980. Both the extremist organizations were proscribed in October 1981. When the man asked Purnima to join the militant underground outfit, it did not sound an absurd proposal to either.

In fact Manipur, which has a matriarchial society, has not only had women enlist for various insurgent organizations fighting a war with the Indian State for liberation, but they have on their own strength conceived and fuelled protest movements of historical significance. In the early 1980s they formed the Manipur Nupi Kanglup (Manipur Women's Organization). On 23 May 1980 as many as 10,000 of its members marched in procession for three days through Imphal to protest against deployment of security forces in the state. They also came out to oppose the promulgation of AFSPA (Armed Forces Special Powers Act 1958), in September 1980. Women protested too against combing operations by security forces to flush out insurgents.[44]

It was the bold protest by naked women in July 2004 that showed the world to what extent women of Manipur are willing to go for a fight dear to them. As hundreds of women came out to demonstrate against the alleged rape and murder of a 32-year-old woman by men of the Assam Rifles, about forty of them shed their clothes and held up banners at the Assam Rifles base and headquarters in Imphal.

Way back in 1904, the women of Manipur had stood up against the British when their men were ordered to fetch timber from a huge distance to rebuild houses of the officers destroyed in a fire. The historical Nupi Lal (Women's War) movement of 1939 is well recorded. The Manipur women, traditionally responsible for the production, selling and marketing of food grain, started Nupi Lal to prevent the export of rice when they faced a shortage of it. Even today, Imphal has the world's only women's bazaar in which they sell handlooms and grain. Ideological conviction and safeguarding their interests have

44. Phanjoubam Tarapot, *Insurgency Movement in Northeastern India*, pp. 82, 89.

always been the driving factor for women activists even if it means resorting to aggressive means.

Purnima too was driven by her own pressing needs. Joining a rebel group meant shelter, food and, above all, security against exploitation. With a gun and uniform she would be able to intimidate people instead of being intimidated by them. No one had ever been good or kind to her. She did not want to be at the receiving end anymore. Besides life as an underground activist could not be worse than what she had lived. 'From the age of nine when my mother went mad, I scrounged for food in dustbins, picked up discarded old clothes left on streets and slept on pavements. I did odd jobs in homes till I found my way to my stepbrother. By then I was eleven and totally unwelcome in his home.'

At sixteen, she was married off to 25-year-old Thanjam Premji, a farmer in Sanjenbam village. He left her four years later with two children and a third on the way. Purnima had no option but to return to her brother's house. She worked as a daily wage labourer, sold vegetables and sat at the loom to weave to support herself and her children. But the money was never enough. Her brother 'wanted to get rid of me and tried to marry me off again'. Purnima was done with marital life so she decided to leave her brother's place. She left her children with her husband and set out for nowhere. 'I needed a place to sleep where no one would chase me away or question me. I decided that the cemetery in Imphal would be the best for me.' Were you not afraid? I ask her. 'I did not care if I lived or died. I had seen so much in life that I was scared of nothing,' she replies.

Over a period of seven years, being fearless and without a care for her life made Purnima a much in demand KCP assassin and extortionist by her camp commanders. Purnima, now known as

Nalini with a KCP registration number, soon carried a reward of Rs 50,000 on her head. Will this disclosure not get you in trouble? I ask as she talks about her work for the rebel outfit. 'There is no visual record of Nalini,' she answers calmly. In any case it would be difficult to connect the present-day Purnima with the KCP militant, assassin and extortionist Nalini.

Today she is known as the benign faith healer of Bethel House Healing Centre at Sanakeithel, a desolate spot in Imphal's Langol Games Village locality. Purnima has discarded the phenak (handwoven wrap-around skirt) and innaphi (shawl) worn by women in Manipur. Instead she wears only track pants and T-shirts. Her long straight hair has been replaced by a close-cropped cut. 'I have done this because all my problems arose because of my being a woman. I don't want to look like one anymore,' she says with quiet determination.

She exchanged her phenak for green combat attire when she began her maiden journey to the KCP camp in the 'hill district'. The man who had persuaded her to join the militant group had introduced her to another girl who was her escort during the two-day trek to the camp. 'We lived in a village. The training centre was just outside the village. This was my first contact with the hill people. They were scantily dressed and had no access to medical aid. They would carry their sick to get medical assistance on stretchers made of bamboo.' Much as she wanted to do something about it, Purnima had a tough training programme to go through. 'There were about fifty of us undergoing training. Fifteen were girls.'

Purnima learnt how to use AK-47 and AK-56 rifles, fire a 9 mm pistol ('they were of Chinese and Japanese make'), put together RDX bombs and secure an area with mines. Besides arms training she was given lessons in disguise, how to melt into a crowd, how to ensure safety of civilians while taking shelter in their home, finance, organizational work and 'Communist political ideology'. With every passing day, Purnima began to appreciate not only the 'discipline of the Red Army' but also their cause. 'I began to see the right of it. The Red Army wanted to bring about a distribution of wealth amongst the people, preserve our culture and teach us how to look after our land. I felt the struggle would bring peace for our troubled people.'

At the end of six months the trainees had to sit for an examination. 'I have never been to school but I topped in this,' she says with pride. Purnima was given a registration number and turned into Junior Private Nalini. From that moment 'I decided that I would do assignments to near perfection'. As the years went by, the assignments became tougher and tougher. In 2005 she was sent to the Assam Rifle camp near village Henglep in Manipur's Churachandpur district as a member of an ambush party of 250 made up of the KCP and another rebel group. 'My task was to give cover to the men who carried out the ambush. I was armed with a gun and Lethode bombs. I used them for self-defence. Between fifteen and twenty of the cadre died.' Her next assignment was a one-hour encounter with the army near Keimai in Manipur's district of Imphal West. 'This was nothing compared to the two-month journey we had to make to the camp in Jiribam,' she says. It was a 'non-stop walk over forested hills' to Jiribam which is on the western border of Manipur adjoining Cachar district of Assam. 'We walked in silence in a single column keeping a gap of about fifteen metres, carrying guns and survival kits. We stopped only at night to eat. I have never experienced such a tough trek,' she recounts.

The real challenge for Purnima was yet to come. She was ordered to accompany a sergeant major, cross the border into Myanmar and open a KCP camp there. After almost three years of living in jungle fatigues, Purnima changed into a phenak and draped an innaphi across her shoulders. 'I hated it but had to do it to disguise myself,' she says. From Jiribam town she and her companion took a bus for an eight-hour drive to Imphal. 'We pretended to be a couple going to Imphal.' The pretending was easy for her comrade 'because he wanted to marry me. But I was going to do no such thing. If there is anything I am scared of it is marriage'.

From Imphal they drove to Moreh, a trading town located on the India–Myanmar border in Manipur's Chandel district. Moreh has for long been a crossover point for rebels from India's northeastern states to Myanmar. Besides the legal import of betel nuts, turmeric, dry ginger and red kidney beans, there is a flourishing clandestine import of drugs and arms. It is a big bazaar for insurgents as well as the folks from surrounding villages. The border town of Tamu on the Myanmar side is about a two-hour walk. Purnima and the other KCP soldier did not choose to walk across. Their destination lay deeper into the forests of Myanmar.

'We hired a tonga and travelled for five days to set up our camp in Myanmar,' says Purnima. But before it could be done, Purnima's ability to negotiate and handle large sums of money was put to test. 'I worked out a deal with the Burmese soldiers by paying them five lakhs. Then I talked to two other rebel groups to allow me to open a camp.' She requisitioned tarpaulin sheets and soon set up a mobile camp. Purnima was made camp commander. This brought on responsibilities she did not have earlier. The camp had about fifty recruits being trained for patrol work and taking part in a daily drill of physical exercise.

Purnima had little choice but to go back to the dress she loathed. 'I had to cross the Moreh post a number of times to recruit people, procure food and medicine and most importantly to arrange for money to run my camp. I pretended to be a petty trader to get past the checkpost.' The disguise part was easier compared to arranging finances. 'I would go to people doing government projects and demand a certain percentage in lieu of KCP protection.' Even while intimidating people, extorting money and while recruiting, Purnima followed a simple rule. 'I never raised my voice and always communicated in a direct straightforward manner. That is why they took me seriously when I told them of the consequences if they did not meet my demand.' She speaks in the same calm manner when she tells me that 'I have never been scared or tired or told a lie' under any situation.

She refused to tell a lie when she went to the house of a KCP renegade on orders from her senior. 'When I called him outside his wife asked me what I wanted. I told her I had orders to kill him because he had betrayed the organization.' The man was frightened out of his wits. He meekly stepped outside and started to walk with Purnima to a dark field. His weeping wife followed, pleading with Purnima to spare his life. When they reached the field 'she flung herself in front to cover him. She told me to shoot her instead. My men tried to pull her away from him so that I could shoot him. In the scuffle her phenak came undone. Her innaphi tore. She was naked but she did not care or even realize it. All she wanted was to save her husband. It struck me then how women want to save lives and here I am, a woman, killing people without a thought.'

As the woman wept and pleaded, the mobile phone in Purnima's pocket rang. 'My commander wanted to know if I was done with the assassination.' Purnima had changed in that one moment. She told a lie. 'I fired in the air and told my senior that I had shot the man.' She then told the man she had been sent to kill to run away with his wife and never be seen again in the area. She told her own men that if they ever sneaked on her, she knew how to deal with them. 'As I turned to leave I saw the man take off his sarong and cover his wife. She looked up at him with tearful eyes and said apologetically that she had not realized she was naked. For the first time I understood what love is and what wonders it can do.'

Sitting in the tin shack that serves as her living quarters, dispensary and office she gestures to the adjacent shack from where comes a constant humming sound. More than seventy men and women are singing or rather chanting in the language of the Kuki and Meitei people of Manipur. 'I cure them with love. I tell them if they love god they will be cured. We sing hymns and pray five times a day. It is all about faith and love,' she explains to me. In 2011, she claims she got the powers to heal people. In 2013, Purnima established the healing centre where she charges Rs 250 to treat a person. 'Some have cancer, some have kidney failure as well as other diseases. They come when they have no hope anywhere else.' According to her, they stay with her for a couple of weeks and are cured. Do you give them these medicines, I ask, pointing to the many bottles of tonics advertised as medicine to gain 'vigour and vitality' and cure cough and pain. 'The cure is revealed to me in my dream. I am told by a godly apparition in white who comes in my dream what medicine to give a particular patient.'

From the night Purnima spared the life of the man she was assigned to assassinate she felt revulsion for the work she had been carrying out. 'I felt that extortion, killing and even recruiting people for militant groups was not good. Violence was not the answer. Love was.' But she also knew that leaving the organization or fleeing was not an easy option. 'Once you are given a registration number, you cannot leave without permission of the leaders. Those who escape are hunted down and killed.' She started to distance herself from her work. 'I told my leaders that I now felt tired and less confident. They thought I wanted to leave and start another faction. I convinced them that was not the case.' Her lack of interest in jobs she routinely took on earlier was soon evident. 'They realized I was no longer the lethal disciplined killer and may slip up while on an assignment. They let me go.' The year was 2008.

But things did not go the way she thought they would. As she was crossing the Moreh checkpost to return to Imphal she was apprehended by some KCP men. 'They thought I was running away without permission.' Purnima was charged with twelve cases. 'I was tortured and hung from the ceiling. They wanted me to confess. They did not believe that I had had enough and God was calling me.' As luck would have it she was spotted by members of the United National Liberation Front (UNLF), another insurgent group. They had shared the camp with KCP in Henglep and 'recognized me. I was well known in the camp'. After they rescued her, they put her through intense interrogation and were convinced 'I was innocent and leaving only because of a calling from God'.

On her return to Imphal, Purnima tried to find work. 'I knew how to embroider so a garment manufacturer employed me for his unit in Tamil Nadu,' she says. Another twist in her life was waiting for her. She ran into trouble with the police and was jailed on charges of child trafficking. She could prove her innocence only after spending twelve days in prison. While there she converted to the Baptist faith. 'Then I started to see a godly figure in my dreams telling me to go out and take care of the sick and spread love.'

After a day of one of my long conversations with her, she asks me to return to her shack late evening. As I walk into her shack, I see her lying motionless in her bed which is veiled by a green net. She is surrounded by the inmates of her centre who are crying uncontrollably. Some are praying. One of her assistants is bent over her, massaging her hands. Another is massaging her legs. She is very ill, they inform me. She cannot talk now, they say. What has happened? I inquire. To my surprise I am told that Purnima goes through this whenever she is overcome by 'negativity' when she absorbs the pain of a sick person. Did she treat a very ill person today? I ask. 'No, it is the pain of her days of violence which you made her relive that has made her ill,' her daughter tells me. It is not an accusation, just an explanation for Purnima taking to her bed and shutting herself off from interaction with anyone. She will be fine in a day or so, her daughter assures me. I turn to leave with the thought that a journey from a destitute to a dreaded militant to a faith healer leaves its scars. Purnima obviously has found a way to come to terms with it.

Epilogue

THE WOMEN PROFILED IN THIS BOOK COME OUT AS STRONG, independent human beings, completely in charge of their lives, making their choices even if it means standing up to their men. This holds good even for those who shared their stories but are not mentioned in this book. To be part of the book was entirely their own decision, albeit taken after much consideration. Most were advised, persuaded and even pressurized not to do so by husbands, sons and brothers. They listened but finally did what they wanted. They came unescorted by their men, choosing on their own a place to meet. When they opened their homes for chats and interactions, they played the gracious hostess ready to start a warm friendship. As they recounted their action-filled days, sometimes with laughter, sometimes with sadness, they ordered the men in the house to churn out refreshments and local delicacies (even in the patriarchal conservative Kashmiri society)! In touching gestures, they offered delicately embroidered kurtas in Kashmir, in Chhattisgarh chunky tribal trinkets, in Assam colourful mekhela chadars, vibrant handwoven shawls in Nagaland and in Manipur attractive phenaks from the exclusive women's market in Imphal, as remembrances to seal the bond of a new-found relationship. Not once during the course of conversations did anyone of them appear defensive about once being part of a banned outfit, joining or for that matter leaving it. Nor was there any sense of guilt or regret at having taken part in killing or subversive activity. All of them are now focused on finding a means to put their lives together after making an exit from an insurgent camp with the same grit, dedication and determination they had when they were in it. All the women do complain that the government has not given them adequate support to rehabilitate themselves. As part of an outlawed militant outfit they never had to worry about money. Now they have to struggle for it to keep their families and homes going, the very aspirational bliss for which they bade goodbye to their leaders and comrades and life underground.

Delving into the minds of women who turn to militancy and join banned outfits is crucial in India today as never before. The role of women insurgents is more pronounced. Women linked to terror groups and outlawed resistance movements are becoming more high-profile. Over time this truth has not only come to be recognized but is also accepted by intelligence agencies as well as those involved in counter-insurgency operations.

Inputs by intelligence agencies reveal that about eight women 'fidayeens' from the Jamat-ud-Dawah (JuD) terror outfit and the Jaish-e-Mohammed (JeM) have infiltrated into India from Pakistan to carry out 'spectacular strikes'. The women have been trained by Pakistan's ISI as honey traps. The JeM, now going by the name Tehreek-e-Azadi Jammu and Kashmir, and the JuD now have women cells.[45]

In September 2015, 38-year old Afsha Jabeen was arrested at Hyderabad after she was deported from the UAE. Afsha was allegedly recruiting Indians online for Daish. She had been under surveillance in India, the UK and the UAE for nine months before she was deported and arrested. In February 2016, the belief that Ishrat Jehan was an LeT operative gained

45. *Times of India*, 16 June 2017.

currency. David Headley, serving sentence in a US prison for his role in the 2008 Mumbai terror attack, testified before a Special Court in Mumbai via video from America that he had been told by the LeT that Ishrat had indeed been recruited by the terrorist outfit.

Encounters between militants and Indian security forces like the one near Ranchi in Chhattisgarh on the night of 18 February 2016 have left behind women insurgents amongst the dead.[46] In March 2018, seven women from the Maoist armed unit were killed in an alleged encounter with the Telengana police. These operatives were ostensibly left behind by their leaders to engage with the security forces while the senior male leaders could escape.[47] This reveals that women cadres are now taking part in ambush and combat operations. The role of women in militant outfits in India is getting more lethal.

The world is seeing the emergence of female human bombs. In November 2015, 26-year-old Hasna Aitboulahcen blew herself up in an apartment days after the 13 November 2015 Paris Daish (Islamic State) terror attacks and earned the dubious distinction of becoming Europe's first female suicide bomber. She detonated her vest of explosives when police stormed the flat she was holed up in with six of her mates.

She was the first to open fire with her Kalashnikov and as the police barged in, she exploded. Minutes before she had tried to fool the police by shouting for help from the window of the flat. Of the four al-Qaeda jihadists who attacked a hotel and restaurant in Burkina Faso in January 2016, killing twenty-three, two reportedly were women. Long before this spate of incidents, on 21 May 1991, the Liberation Tigers of

46. PTI, 19 February 2016.

47. *Indian Express*, 4 March 2018.

Tamil Eelam (LTTE), a lethal militant separatist organization based in Sri Lanka, used Dhanu, a woman suicide bomber to assassinate Rajiv Gandhi in Tamil Nadu. As the book reveals, women militants in India unhesitatingly and fearlessly follow orders from their commanders. It is another matter that ideology (Maoists in Chhattisgarh) and religion (in Kashmir) may not allow for women human bombs. But if ordered, women cadres most likely will go ahead.

Modern counter-terrorism institutions like the National Security Guard (NSG), the Federal Contingency Deployment Force tasked to tackle all facets of terrorism in the country and the National Investigation Agency (NIA) established to combat terror in India would do well to begin an exclusive study of women terrorists. Security forces who encounter terrorists at border frontlines (the Indian Army, BSF, CRPF besides) and the police have to be equipped and trained to handle women in the insurgent cadre and areas under the sway of an armed uprising. Before embarking on this, efforts have to be undertaken to understand such women.

Dealing with militant women suspects can be a tricky business. While it is becoming increasingly important to note that women suspects in militancy-inflicted areas can no longer be dismissed as innocents by security forces, it is as imperative to ensure that innocent women are not harassed during searches or taken advantage of in the name of security concerns. This calls for security forces introducing women personnel in their ranks for search, seek and interrogation operations.

Agencies involved in counter-terrorism operations have to craft women-specific strategies to prevent them from enlisting as insurgents and as importantly, from returning to militant organizations after coming over-ground. In the case of surrendered women insurgents, the government has to ensure effective implementation of its rehabilitation schemes, including financial rewards and aid. Delivery failure on this score leaves them feeling shortchanged and in want. After a taste of empowerment such women hate the idea of being dependent on others. In such a situation, many contemplate a return to a camp where food and shelter is a given. That is why this is far more important in the context of women insurgents than their male counterparts. It is time for counter-terrorism and intelligence agencies to go past labels as they come across women militants. Instead of stopping at slotting them under the generic term 'terrorists' they should study them as a class different from their male comrades. Given the crucial role they play in the operational success of underground outfits, they have to be factored in when crafting counter-terrorism strategy at an institutional level.

While women cadres are a motivated and dedicated daredevil lot, their mindset is not completely similar to that of male terrorists. Nor are the reasons that lead them underground. Their motivation, aspirations, perspective on being part of violent banned outfits, their take on the work assigned to them, the threshold level of wanting to quit a furtive life as well as their ardent longing for a life beyond needs to be studied. Only after this will it be possible to draw up an approach on how to engage with them and more importantly, prevent their flow into insurgent groups. It is imperative to read them as persons with varying behaviour patterns and characteristics.

I hope this book will contribute to the evolution of effective policies to give viable options to women in India being targeted by insurgent outfits to enlist and also to those who come over-ground.

Acknowledgements

THERE ARE MANY WHO HAVE CONTRIBUTED TO MAKE this book possible, but regrettably I can name only a few. Most of the people who assisted and facilitated my search for women insurgents have, for understandable reasons, requested anonymity. Amongst them are members of still active underground outfits, one-time militants, former as well as serving, senior and junior officials from the different security forces, from secret agencies, intelligence-gathering agencies, court functionaries, men of the judiciary and locals in various places. Some have provided an insight into the subject of the book by relating their fieldwork experiences to me, some have given me access to records and files, sparing me official formality, others have trustingly passed on their contacts, while many have silently pointed in a direction that has led me to the protagonists of this book. Many have gone out of their way and helped in travel to remote villages. Some have put in a word for me with their friends, associates and one-time comrades who figure in the book. Each one of them is a vital link in a chain that is essential for a venture such as this. Though some of us are not likely to meet again, I can never forget them for lending a hand in the making of this book. My sincere thanks to them for all they have done for me.

It was the enthusiastic response of my one-time colleague and friend Debashish Mukerji to the subject of the book, when it was only a germ of an idea, which propelled me to start work on it. He encouraged me right through the endeavour. He goaded me on when I hit rock-bottom in tracing women insurgents or was distressed at a failed rendezvous. He has shared my excitement when I returned successful. He patiently heard my adventures and then sanely advised that instead of revelling in them, I immediately put pen to paper. His objective comments gave me the confidence to carry on. I am thankful to him. I also wish to thank senior journalist Raj Chengappa who on hearing about my seemingly never-ending research trips cautioned that I not fall into the trap reporters often do, of obsessively collecting information and never getting down to writing the book.

Journalist comrades, R.C. Ganjoo, Ira Jha and Sunzu Bachaspatimayum gave me immense help when they kindly agreed to accompany me on my journey to remote destinations in their native Jammu and Kashmir, Chhattisgarh and Manipur respectively. Not only did they make good guides but also allowed me to take advantage of the hospitality of their friends and family on the way. They doubled as keen translators and helped establish trust and a friendship of sorts with people the book is about. Thanks for being with me during the rough but fun times we had on our trips. For the sake of our four-decade-old friendship, Shalini Dewan, former Director, United Nation Information Centre for India, graciously agreed to give me days of her vacation to meticulously go through the manuscript and come up with constructive suggestions. Many thanks to her.

My husband Vineet's contribution to my book project needs special mention. He began with outlining the security risk involved and ended with becoming my travel companion. Not once did he grumble about the arduous rail and road trips during which a good meal and comfortable bed were often difficult to come by. Nor did he complain about the tireless assault by mosquitoes, bugs and insects in the thick vegetations we met on our forays outside cities, including the toxic bite by a winged creature during an Assam excursion. It gave him high fever for days and a deep wound which took more than a month to heal. I was glad to have him by my side in dark and lonely and unfamiliar surroundings. He turned out to be a big help in making friends with the women insurgents. One of them chose to reveal her sinister operations to him instead of me on one of the walks the two took during our stay with her. I will always fondly remember what he has done for me.

I am fortunate to have found an editor like Renuka Chatterjee who responded enthusiastically to my manuscript right after the initial read and has since worked meticulously to shape it while remaining sensitive to nuances and my style of narrative. Many thanks to her for providing a stress-free working relationship.